Sailing the Sweetwater Seas

Also by George D. Jepson

Crash Boat: Rescue and Peril in the Pacific During World War II

Quarterdeck: Maritime Literature & Art Review

Sailing the Sweetwater Seas

WOODEN BOATS AND SHIPS ON THE GREAT LAKES, 1817–1940

GEORGE D. JEPSON

WoodenBoat

BROOKLIN, MAINE

SHERIDAN HOUSE

ESSEX, CONNECTICUT

WoodenBoat
◄ S**HERIDAN** H**OUSE** ►

An imprint of Globe Pequot, the trade division of
The Rowman & Littlefield Publishing Group, Inc.
4501 Forbes Blvd., Ste. 200
Lanham, MD 20706
www.rowman.com

Distributed by NATIONAL BOOK NETWORK

British Library Cataloguing-in-Publication Information available

Library of Congress Cataloging-in-Publication Data

Names: Jepson, George D., 1944– author.
Title: Sailing the sweetwater seas : wooden boats and ships on the Great
  Lakes, 1817–1940 / George D. Jepson.
Other titles: Wooden boats and ships on the Great Lakes, 1817–1940
Description: Essex, Connecticut : Sheridan House, 2023. | Includes
  bibliographical references and index. | Summary: "The story of the Great
  Lakes ships and boats on which the United States, barely decades old,
  moved to the country's middle and beyond, established a robust
  industrial base, and became a world power, despite enduring a bloody
  Civil War. In text and photographs, this book tells the story of a
  bygone era, of mariners and Mackinaw boats, schooners and steamboats,
  all helping to advance the young nation westward"— Provided by
  publisher.
Identifiers: LCCN 2023002807 (print) | LCCN 2023002808 (ebook) | ISBN
  9781493072279 (cloth) | ISBN 9781493077649 (epub)
Subjects: LCSH: Ships, Wooden—Great Lakes (North America)—History. |
  Wooden boats—Great Lakes (North America)—History. | Merchant
  ships—Great Lakes (North America)—History. | Seafaring life—Great
  Lakes (North America)—History. | Sailors—Great Lakes (North
  America)—Biography. | Inland navigation—Great Lakes (North
  America)—History.
Classification: LCC VM144 .J477 2023 (print) | LCC VM144 (ebook) | DDC
  623.82/070977—dc23/eng/20230413
LC record available at https://lccn.loc.gov/2023002807
LC ebook record available at https://lccn.loc.gov/2023002808

Printed in India

Contents

MINNESOTA
Port Arthur
Ft. William
ONTARIO
Michipicoten
Isle Royale
LAKE SUPERIOR
QUÉBEC
Apostle Islands
Keweenaw Point
CANADA
Duluth
Houghton
Boraga
Superior
Ontonagon
L'Anse
Ashland
Marquette
Munising
Sault Ste Marie
Killarney
Soo Canal
MICHIGAN
Manistique
St. Ignace
Escanaga
Strait of Mackinac
Parry Sound
Mackinaw
Beaver Island
Calcits
Georgian Bay
Menominee
Potoskey
Alpena
St. Lawrence River
WISCONSIN
LAKE HURON
Green Bay
Traverse City
Midland
Frankfort
Owen Sound
Manitowoc
Manistee
Osh Kosh
Ludington
Watertown
Sheboygan
Goderich
Toronto
LAKE ONTARIO
USA
MICHIGAN
Bay City
Oswego
Hamilton
Milwaukee
Muskegon
Niagara Falls
Rochester
Port Huron
Port
Welland Canal
Racine
Sarnia
Burwell
Port Colborne
New York State Barge Canal (Erie Canal)
Holland
Buffalo
Saugatuck
Detroit
NEW YORK
Chicago
Benton Harbor
Windsor
LAKE ERIE
Erie
Sanitary & Ship Canal
Michigan City
Conneaut
Gary
Ashtabula
Toledo
Cleveland
ILLINOIS
INDIANA
Sandusky
Lorain
PENNSYLVANIA
OHIO
LAKE MICHIGAN

Preface and Acknowledgments

The seeds for *Sailing the Sweetwater Seas* were planted in the late 1940s and early 1950s, many years before I considered a career as a writer. I was born in Marquette in Michigan's Upper Peninsula, on the shore of Lake Superior. Until I was six, I only knew the "big lake"—dark blue and beautiful on sunny days. On stormy days, the color turned an ominous bluish-gray punctuated with white caps as towering waves roared ashore. Other times, fog, a gray-white murk, descended on the town, and the foghorn on Lighthouse Point sounded its full-throated warnings to shipping.

Living near the shore, I watched longships, or "ore boats," with their pilothouses forward and rear stacks trailing smoke on the horizon, inbound for Marquette's two harbors to load iron ore for delivery down the lakes. These freighters, stretching up to 600' in those days, would eventually ease alongside the immense ore docks in either the upper or lower harbor. Chutes on the docks would lower to hatch openings in the decks below, and pockets of taconite pellets would fill the ships' holds by the ton. Then, riding low in the water, they steamed east to the Soo Locks, down Lake Huron to Lake Erie and Cleveland, Ohio, or down Lake Michigan to Gary, Indiana, where mills melted the pellets into steel.

It was a magical time for a boy.

In mid-September 1951, we moved to Lower Michigan. As we drove along US Highway 2 in the UP, bordering the sandy Lake Michigan shore, the water's aquamarine color looked pale compared to Superior's deep blue. Crossing the Straits of Mackinac on a car ferry (the Mackinac Bridge was still six years in the future), I saw Lake Huron for the first time. I was sad leaving the Upper Peninsula and Lake Superior, but the next two summers, I returned to the Big Lake, staying with my grandparents across from McCarty's Cove.

Memories from those early years in my life stayed with me, and decades later, as a freelance writer specializing in maritime topics, I queried

WoodenBoat magazine editor Matthew Murphy, pitching an article on the wooden schooners that sailed the Great Lakes in the nineteenth century. Matt responded affirmatively, and that initial story evolved into a series. Side-wheel and propeller steamers came after the schooners, followed by the early bulk freighters that carried iron ore from Lake Superior ports down the lakes, predecessors to the mammoth freighters today that stretch to 1,000' in length. Lastly, we featured the first recreational boats on the Great Lakes.

While researching these articles, two preeminent Great Lakes historians kindly introduced me to the rich resources documenting the history of the purpose-built ships sailing the Great Lakes from just after the War of 1812 to the 1930s. C. Patrick Labadie, maritime historian and underwater archaeologist, shared his collection of research materials, including period photographs, and reviewed my early manuscripts. Henry Barkhausen, a legend who sailed aboard one of the last working schooners on the Great Lakes in the 1930s and dedicated much of his long life to maritime history, offered much-appreciated direction and encouragement.

Ken Pott, then executive director of the Heritage Museum and Cultural Center at St. Joseph, Michigan, generously shared his original research about the historic scow-schooner *Rockaway*. Additionally, Ken opened the museum's archives documenting the Truscott Boat Manufacturing Company in St. Joseph.

At the Marquette Regional History Center, Rosemary Michelin, now retired as the librarian in the John M. Longyear Library, was highly supportive, opening the archives on several occasions as I researched my articles. And Patti Montgomery Reinert, executive director of the Michigan Maritime Museum in South Haven, kindly opened the archives in the Marialyce Canonie Great Lakes Research Library in the old Keeper's House overlooking the iconic barn-red South Haven Light.

Finally, Don La Barre, head of Special Collections at the Alpena County George N. Fletcher Public Library, graciously made images from the library's Great Lakes Maritime Collection, including many from the C. Patrick Labadie Collection, available to me. Over the years, Marlo Broad, then working in Special Collections for the library, was instrumental in locating and providing images of historic Great Lakes ships illustrating the *WoodenBoat* articles.

One day, I received an email from Matt Murphy suggesting that the articles would make a book—a gratifying thought that I tucked away for another time. Then, after Lyons Press, an imprint of Globe Pequot, published *Crash Boat: Rescue and Peril in the Pacific During World War II*, which I co-authored with Earl A. McCandlish, that time arrived. Rick Rinehart, the executive editor of Globe Pequot, acquired the book for the Sheridan House imprint.

Sailing the Sweetwater Seas: Wooden Boats and Ships on the Great Lakes, 1817–1940 is based on my *WoodenBoat* articles, with new material and illustrations. Along the way, I also learned more about my family's modest roles in the history of the Great Lakes, beginning in the years after the Civil War. As work progressed on this volume, marine historian and artist Robert McGreevy came aboard with his beautifully executed drawings and paintings.

The Great Lakes (Superior, Michigan, Huron, Erie, and Ontario), sometimes called the "Inland Seas," were the nation's first superhighway. The Jesuit missionaries, arriving at Georgian Bay on Lake Huron in the early 1600s, christened the linked lakes "seas of sweet water." They were mystified that, unlike the oceans, there was no salty taste when they sipped the water. So, that's how the book's title came about.

Part One tells the stories of the wooden working vessels that sailed the sweetwater seas and the shipwrights who designed and built them. This section also remembers the New Englanders, immigrants, and celebrities like Charles Dickens and Captain Frederick Marryat who flocked aboard narrow packet boats on the Erie Canal, bound for Buffalo and onward across the lakes.

Part Two turns to the late nineteenth century and the evolution of wooden boats on the Great Lakes, the men who designed and built recreational vessels, a notorious "pirate" on Lake Michigan, and, finally, to legendary maritime historian Henry Barkhausen, who dedicated much of his long life to preserving the history and memories of the boats, ships, and mariners who sailed them over more than a century.

There are always unsung individuals who make a book possible. At *WoodenBoat*, I am grateful to Matt Murphy for his confidence and support for the Great Lakes articles. I am indebted to *WoodenBoat* editors Tom Jackson, Karen Wales, and Maynard Bray, for their oversight and deft edits. At Globe Pequot, Rick Rinehart and Brittany Stoner (acquisitions editor aptly nicknamed "Hurricane" for the way she approaches her projects), guided me through the production process with the Rowman & Littlefield Publishing Group. Finally, none of this would have happened without the constant support and encouragement from my wife, Amy, who read and commented on every word.

—George D. Jepson
Autumn 2023

The Erie Canal and Beyond

On the morning of Wednesday, October 26, 1825, New York governor DeWitt Clinton waited to lead a parade from the Greek Revival courthouse in Buffalo, then a small village on Lake Erie's eastern shore, to the Erie Canal to officially open the waterway. After eight years under construction, the canal now connected the Great Lakes with the Atlantic Ocean via the Hudson River. The day had dawned with a chill in the air, but the countryside, splashed with glorious autumn colors under brilliantly sunny skies, uplifted everyone's spirits. Red, white, and blue bunting and the Stars and Stripes draped on the wood-frame homes and businesses along the village's wide dirt streets added to the festive air.

New York governor DeWitt Clinton by American artist Rembrandt Peale. PUBLIC DOMAIN

Earlier that morning, an estimated three thousand revelers, most of the village's twenty-four hundred inhabitants, others from nearby communities, and visiting dignitaries, had assembled in the park in front of the courthouse. Then, just before 9:00 a.m., an artillery salute launched the procession and merrymaking. With the Buffalo Band of Music leading the way, Clinton, who had provided the impetus for the canal project for over fifteen years, and the crowd marched down Main Street toward the Canal Basin. Reaching the canal, Clinton and James Tallmadge Jr., the state's lieutenant governor, climbed aboard the *Seneca Chief,* a long, narrow wooden packet boat designed to carry passengers. After speeches by the governor and worthies from across the state concluded, a thirty-two-pound cannon boomed, signaling the waterway's official opening and setting off a rolling thunder along the 363-mile-long canal and the Hudson River to New York City.

As the distant thud of a cannon reached each town, it, in turn, fired its own gun. Finally, when the last battery fired at New York Harbor, the message was sent back up the chain to Buffalo. "The Grand Salute was commenced at precisely ten o'clock, and the return gun was heard at twenty minutes past one," according to the *Buffalo Emporium and General Advertiser* the following Saturday. Hence, the sound took three hours and twenty minutes to reach New York and return to Buffalo. Among the cannons making the salute, several had served aboard Admiral Oliver Perry's ships during his triumph over the British on Lake Erie during the War of 1812.

With white powder smoke drifting in the air, four gray horses pulled the *Seneca Chief* from its moorings, brass bands struck up a lively patriotic tune, and the boat embarked on a ten-day journey to New York and more celebrations amid raucous cheers and small arms discharging into the air. At least three other boats—a second packet and two freight vessels—followed the governor's boat. Two wooden kegs were stowed on the *Seneca Chief*'s foredeck, containing "sweetwater" from Lake Erie, which Clinton planned to pour into the Atlantic Ocean when he arrived in New York.

Buffalo Harbour from the Village in 1825, a lithograph by George Catlin, published in the Committee of the Common Canal of the City of New York Memoir and presented to New York City mayor William Paulding at the Celebration of the Completion of the New York Canals. IMAGE FROM "EXTRA-ILLUSTRATED" EDITION OF THE MEMOIR IN NEW YORK PUBLIC LIBRARY DIGITAL COLLECTIONS, PUBLIC DOMAIN

While Clinton's packet moved slowly eastward, the Buffalo procession returned to the court-house for more speeches. Afterward, the crowd dispersed to various public houses where merrymakers raised toasts. At the Eagle Tavern, the party drank to DeWitt Clinton, according to the *Buffalo Journal* on October 27, 1825: "The completion of the Erie Canal is the best commentary on his judgment—while contemplating its usefulness, posterity will never fail to associate the name of its projector." That evening, the Eagle Tavern hosted "a most splendid ball."

By the time the *Seneca Chief* left Buffalo, portions of the Erie Canal had already been in use, gaining considerable popularity among travelers and businesses. The first boat to traverse the entire length of the canal, the *Benjamin Wright*, arrived in Buffalo the same day Clinton departed aboard the *Seneca Chief*, with both vessels passing one another at some point.

During their eastward journey to New York, twenty towns welcomed the *Seneca Chief* and the accompanying boats with joyous celebrations. Finally, the governor's party reached Albany, the state capital, on Wednesday, November 2, where spirited crowds gathered along the waterfront to greet the arriving boats with more cheers. After several events, including a formal assembly with national officials and a banquet, Clinton's flotilla, escorted by a

The Erie Canal officially opened on October 26, 1825. New York governor DeWitt Clinton, the driving force behind the project, led the opening ceremonies in Buffalo and over the next ten days rode the canal boat *Seneca Chief* to the Hudson River and New York City. PUBLIC DOMAIN

fleet of eight steamboats spewing sparks and black smoke from their stacks, embarked on its final leg down the Hudson the following morning. On Friday, November 4, the fleet arrived at New York, where cannons roared, church bells rang, crowds in the thousands cheered, and more flag- and bunting-draped vessels waited. The entire flotilla proceeded past Brooklyn and through the narrows to Sandy Hook Bay, where Clinton, aboard the steamer *Washington*, hefted a keg to his shoulder and poured Lake Erie's fresh water into the salty Atlantic, officially wedding the Great Lakes to the Atlantic Ocean.

—◦◦✕◦◦—

The Erie Canal, an extraordinary engineering feat for its time, once disparaged and dubbed "Clinton's Ditch" or "Clinton's Folly," initially connected four Great Lakes (Erie, Huron, Michigan, and Superior) via the Hudson River with the Atlantic. Completion in 1828 of the Oswego Canal, a branch of the Erie Canal, and the Welland Canal in 1833 linked Lake Ontario with Lake Erie and

Governor DeWitt Clinton pours water from Lake Erie into the Atlantic Ocean, wedding the two bodies while commemorating the opening of the Erie Canal at New York. PUBLIC DOMAIN

the Atlantic. Travel on the canals was less demanding than overland routes, less expensive, and faster, even at 4 miles per hour.

Buffalo, the Erie Canal's Western Terminus, grew from a small backwater village to a major port

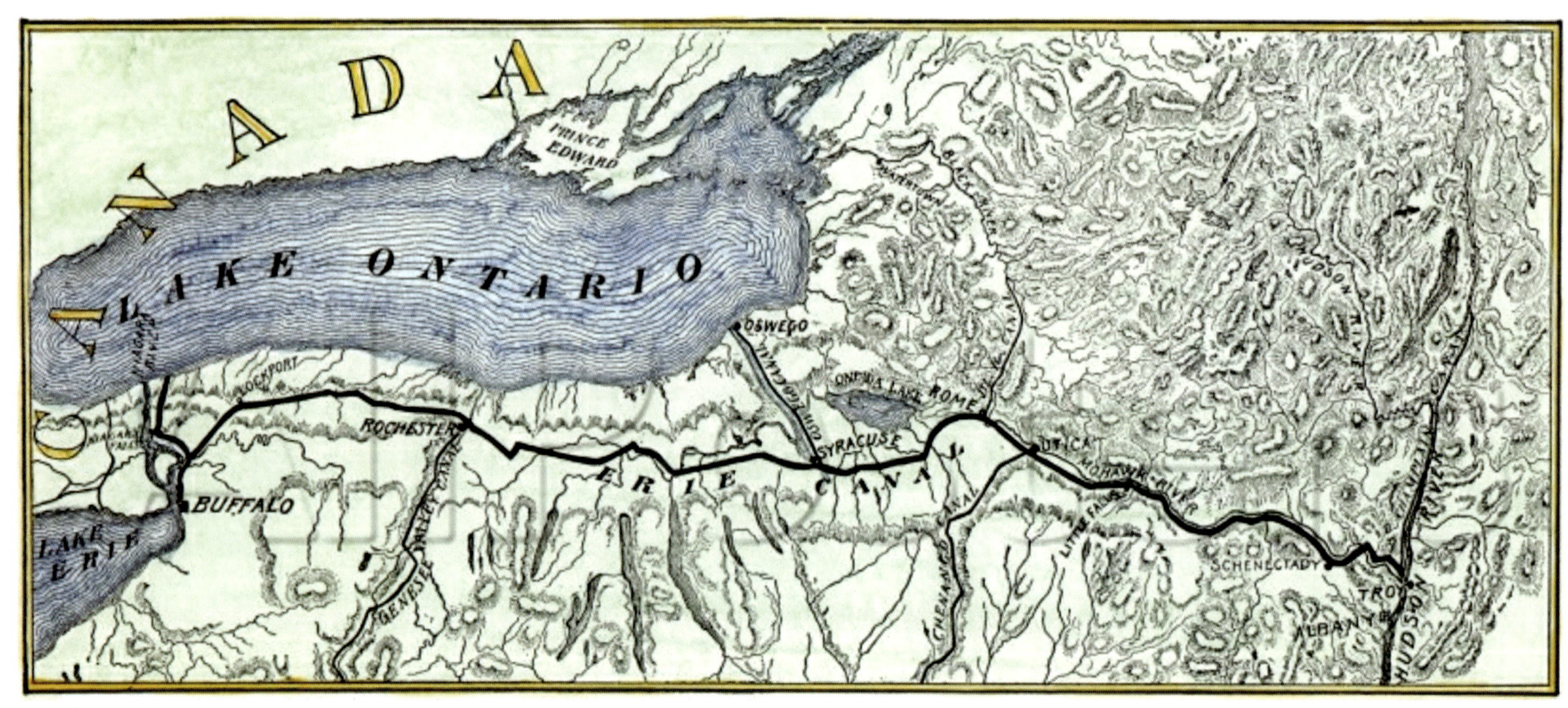

A New York State map, circa 1840, shows the Erie Canal stretching from Troy on the Hudson River in the east to Buffalo on Lake Erie in the west.

city. Hundreds of thousands of New Englanders and immigrants from Scandinavia and Europe flooded the waterway. Arriving at Buffalo, they clambered aboard sailing vessels (primarily schooners and barks) and steamers with their worldly possessions, filled with hopes and dreams, bound over the lakes for the future states of Ohio, Michigan, Illinois, and Wisconsin. Twelve years after the completion of the Erie Canal, Captain Frederick Marryat, Charles Dickens's literary contemporary and friend, sailed to America from England aboard the packet *Quebec*. The former British Royal Navy officer-turned-novelist spent two years traveling the country. During his journeys, he compiled his *Diary in America* and described his westward trip on the Erie Canal and the Oswego Canal (see sidebar on right). In the decades ahead, America and the world came to appreciate the Great Lakes and the boats and ships that plied the sweet waters.

CAPTAIN FREDERICK MARRYAT ON THE CANALS

In 1837, Captain Frederick Marryat arrived in America. During his westward journey on the Erie and the Oswego Canals, he recorded in his diary his time on the canals, beginning in Utica.

Captain Frederick Marryat, circa 1826, by English artist John Simpson. WIKIPEDIA, PUBLIC DOMAIN

Set off for Oswego in a canal boat; it was called a packet-boat because it did not carry merchandise, but was a very small affair, about 50' long by 8' wide. The captain of her was, however, in his own opinion, no small affair; he puffed and swelled until he looked larger than his boat. This personage, as soon as we under weigh, sat down in the narrow cabin, before a small table; sent for his writing-desk, which was about the size of [a] street organ, and, like himself, no small affair; ordered a bell to be rung in our ears to summon the passengers; and, then, taking down the names of four or five people, received the enormous sum of ten dollars passage-money. He then locked his desk with a key large enough for a street-door, ordered his steward to remove it, and went on deck to walk just three feet and return again. After all, there is nothing like being a captain.

Although many of the boats are laid up, there is still considerable traffic on this canal. We passed Rome, a village of two thousand inhabitants, at which number it has for many years been nearly stationary. This branch of the canal is, of course, cut through the levels, and we passed through swamps and wild forests; here and there some few acres were cleared, and a log-house was erected, looking very solitary and forlorn, surrounded by the stumps of the trees which had been felled, and which now lay corded up on the banks of the canal, ready to be disposed of. Wild and dreary as the country is, the mass of forest is gradually receding, and occasionally some solitary tree is left standing, throwing out its wide arms, and appearing as if in lamentation at its separation from its companions, with whom for centuries it has been in close friendship.

Extremes meet: as I look down from the roof of the boat upon the giants of the forest, which had for so many centuries reared their heads undisturbed, but now lay prostrate before civilisation, the same feelings were conjured up in my mind as when I have, in my wanderings, surveyed such fragments of dismembered empires as the ruins of Carthage or of Rome. There the reign of Art was over, and Nature had resumed her sway—here Nature was deposed, and about to resign her throne to the usurper Art. By the bye, the mosquitoes of this district have reaped some benefit from the cutting of the canal here. Before these impervious forest retreats were thus pierced, they could not have tasted human blood; for ages it must have been unknown to them, even by tradition; and if they taxed all other boats on the canal as they did, ours, a *canal share* with them must be considerably above par, and highly profitable.

At five o'clock we arrived at Syracuse. I do detest these old names vamped up. Why do not the Americans take the Indian names? They need not be so very scrupulous about it; they have robbed the Indians of everything else.

After you pass Syracuse, the country wears a more populous and inviting appearance. Salina is a village built upon a salt spring, which has the greatest flow of water yet known, and this salt spring is the cause of the improved appearance of the country; the banks of the canal, for three miles, are lined with buildings for the boiling down of the salt water, which is supplied by a double row of pipes. Boats are constantly employed up and down the canal, transporting wood for the supply of the furnaces . . . Two million bushels of salt are boiled down every year: it is packed in barrels, and transported by the canals and lakes to Canada, Michigan, Chicago, and the far West.

The first sixty miles of this canal (I get on very slow with my description, but canal traveling is very slow), is through flat, swampy forest, is without a lock; but after you pass Syracuse, you have to descend by locks to the Oswego river, and the same at every rapid of the river; in all, there is a fall of one hundred and sixty feet.

The country round the Oswego is fertile and beautiful, and the river, with its islands, falls, and rapids, very picturesque. At one p.m. we arrived at the town of Oswego, on Lake Ontario; I was pleased with the journey, although, what with ducking to bridges, bites from mosquitoes, and the constant blowing of their unearthly horn with only one note, and which one must have been borrowed from the gamut of the infernal regions, I had had enough of it.

WORKING VESSELS EVOLVE

Beginning around 1840 and stretching beyond the 1870s, inland (shoal-draft, centerboard) schooners came to port laden with trade goods that broadened industrial development in the Midwest. This photograph depicts a typical day in 1870 on the St. Clair River at Sarnia, Ontario, Canada. Note more masts across the river in Port Huron, Michigan.
COURTESY OF THUNDER BAY NATIONAL MARINE SANCTUARY, C. PATRICK LABADIE COLLECTION

Schooners
THE HEARTLAND SAILS
INTO THE INDUSTRIAL AGE

The American Civil War was still fresh in the minds of Americans when the two-masted scow-schooner *Rockaway* was launched on November 13, 1866, at Oswego, New York. Built in the Chandler, Alford & Co. shipyard, she began a commercial career in the lumber trade that was to span twenty-five years. She was large for her type, with an overall length (LOA) of 111', a 24' beam, and drawing a mere 6½'. The *Oswego Commercial Advertiser and Times* described her as "staunch and trim . . . sliding gracefully down the ways and out into her native element."

After the War of 1812 ended, shipyards along the shores of the Great Lakes were busy building wooden vessels until the 1880s. Almost every town supported one or more yards buzzing with activity, providing significant employment opportunities as new settlements grew. Farmers sold abundant hardwood stands to the yards, which assisted them in making land payments. In the winter, they hauled timber to the shipyards with their horses.

Schooners working on the Great Lakes during this period were the eighteen-wheelers of their time. The opening of the Erie Canal in 1825 spurred their proliferation and evolution, in turn expanding commerce. The Midwest was heavily forested. Roads, where they existed, were unpaved, and railroads were years from reaching any location beyond the most populated cities. Covered wagons—a westward expansion icon—played a significant role in winning the Midwest. Still, the Great Lakes schooners, with their speed and enormous carrying capacity, were keys to the region's development.

Many of these schooners had a yard on the foremast to fly a loose-footed square sail called a "course," and a triangular topsail above it called a "raffee." Although pure square-rigged vessels also sailed the Great Lakes, schooners rigged with fore-and-aft sails far outnumbered them. The latter were easier to handle, better sailing to windward in confined waters, carried smaller crews, and had booms that could be shifted to facilitate loading and unloading cargo.

There were also barks (or barques) and barkentines (or barquentines) working on the Great Lakes. These three-masted vessels were often loosely referred to as schooners. On barks, however, the foremast and sometimes their main masts carried square sails. Barkentine foremasts carried square sails, while the main and mizzen masts had fore-and-aft rigs. Barkentines were proportionally long and narrow, allowing them to navigate the

canals. There were also two-masted, square-rigged brigs and brigantines on the Lakes but in significantly fewer numbers than schooners.

The bark *American Union*—186.48' LOA, with a 33.16' beam and a 13.14' depth—was launched at Ira Lafrinier's shipyard in Cleveland, Ohio, in 1862. Underway, she would have been a stunning sight with her clipper bow adorned with a figurehead, a square stern, massive spars, and the sails on her three masts filled with a sea breeze.

Built a year into the Civil War, *American Union* was technically a barkentine. Frequently laden with grain, she sailed for thirty-three years on the Great Lakes. Celebrated for her speed between ports, she was stranded by a squall off Presque Isle, Michigan, on May 6, 1894, and wrecked two weeks later by another more significant storm before being salvaged.

By the 1820s, the demand for these shoal-draft, centerboard schooners and barks, built to navigate shallow waters and the sandbars that lie at the mouths of lakeside rivers, had caused a great number of port towns to spring into being. Manistee,

The Barque *American Union* off Presque Isle, Michigan, 1869, by Robert McGreevy (oil on canvas, 15 × 25 inches, private collection).
© ROBERT MCGREEVY

Michigan, is a prime example. In less than thirty years, Manistee experienced a meteoric rise from little more than three lumber camps at the mouth of a river to becoming a major shipbuilding center and port of trade, following only Chicago and Milwaukee in importance.

The Great Lakes were vast highways on which manufactured goods, such as tools, clothing, rope, and farm implements, were shipped in from points east in return for local commodities, including iron ore, coal, stone, lumber, fence posts, shingles, produce, and grain.

During the 1980s, maritime historian Kenneth R. Pott launched an archaeological study of the *Rockaway*'s remains in Lake Michigan. *Rockaway* was one of the largest scow-schooners to sail the Great Lakes. Her story is, perhaps, the most complete of any Great Lakes schooner on record. While her bones have long fallen to the bottom of Lake Michigan, she speaks volumes for the fleets that served the development of the midwestern region of the United States.

The schooner *George J. Boyce*, flying a triangular "raffee" sail on her foremast, had an LOA of 136'10", and a beam of 30'. From 1882 to 1900, she sailed primarily between Manitowoc, Wisconsin, and Grand Haven, Michigan. COURTESY OF THUNDER BAY NATIONAL MARINE SANCTUARY, C. PATRICK LABADIE COLLECTION

Three types of schooners sailed the Great Lakes: the scow, the canaller, and the traditionally designed hull. Falling between these was the "mosquito," a diminutive amalgam often considered by captains of the larger sailing vessels and steamers to be a nuisance.

SCOW-SCHOONERS

The scow-schooner was a primary variation of the schooner used in large numbers on the Great Lakes. These vessels had flat bottoms and hard bilges, though many had traditional bluff schooner bows and carried either two or three masts. Scow-schooners ran the gamut from rough or plain-looking vessels to those with more refined lines and finishes. Some carried bowsprits. The 1885 edition of the *List of Merchant Vessels of the United States* stated that "The distinctive line between the scow and the regular-built [traditional design] schooner . . . would seem to be determined by the shape of the bilge, the scow having in all cases the angular bilge instead of the curved (futtock) bilge of the ordinary vessel."

There are no known photographs of *Rockaway*. However, photographs of a similar-looking vessel (though not a true sister ship), the *Helen*, endure. Originally built in 1874 in Milwaukee and named *Ulster*, she was slightly smaller than *Rockaway*. Renamed *Helen* in 1881, she had an LOA of 90', a 23' beam, and a 7' draft. The schooner, which foundered off Muskegon, Michigan, on November 18, 1886, was discovered in September 2002. Unfortunately, little more is known of her short life history.

Rockaway was at the pinnacle of scow-schooner design. Although, as we shall see, her premature loss in 1891 was a blow to her owners, she became a priceless window into the past when she was discovered on September 29, 1983, after the *Captain Nichols*, a charter fishing boat based in South Haven, Michigan, snagged her anchor on the wreck. In addition to significant sections of the vessel's hull, a wide range of artifacts was discovered, including a pile of chain, hand tools, fastenings, rigging gear, nautical items, and the ship's wheel. Ken Pott championed the project,

There are no known photographs of *Rockaway*, considered the pinnacle of scow-schooner design. However, the scow-schooner *Helen*, née *Ulster*, had lines that were similar to those of *Rockaway*. COURTESY OF THUNDER BAY NATIONAL MARINE SANCTUARY, C. PATRICK LABADIE COLLECTION

believing the site could "provide information about life aboard a late-19th-century Great Lakes scow-schooner . . . for which the historical record was limited in detailed information."

For five seasons, Pott and his team dove on the wreck site sixty-five feet below Lake Michigan's surface, collecting measurements, taking photographs, and generally gathering pertinent information about the nineteenth-century vessel. All the while, the team took extreme care not to disturb the integrity of the wreck and the surrounding site.

Brower A. Morgan was the lead shipwright for Chandler, Alford & Co., who oversaw *Rockaway*'s construction. As a young man, Morgan had gone to work in Oswego shipyards. By the time her keel was laid, Morgan was forty-two years old, and a designer as well as a master carpenter. He continued in his trade in Oswego shipyards for nearly another forty years.

The day after her launching on November 14, 1866, this big scow-schooner sailed for Shannonville, Ontario, where she collected a load of cedar and four barrels of herring and returned to Oswego. Over the next quarter-century, she performed yeoman service for her owners, carrying various cargoes. "The ship's sailing qualities were complemented by a length, beam, and depth ratio which afforded a significant carrying volume, above and below decks, for low density bulk cargoes," said Pott.

On November 16, 1891, *Rockaway* sailed with a crew of six from Ludington, Michigan, bound for Benton Harbor on the state's southwestern shore, heavily laden above and below decks with two hundred thousand board feet of green lumber. By all accounts, this was to be her final passage of the season before being put up for the coming winter. Captain Ole Thompson—a Norwegian immigrant and a one-quarter owner of the vessel—was in command. By afternoon, a day later, *Rockaway* had completed nearly three-quarters of the 130-mile voyage when westerly winds rapidly reached gale-force intensity, creating high seas.

"A vain attempt to work toward the west shore resulted in the [ship's] main canvas being 'blown to shreds' and the loss of the fore-boom and gaff sails," wrote Pott in 2001 (*The Wreck of the Rockaway: The Historical Archaeology of a Great Lakes Schooner*). "It was not long before high winds and freezing temperatures rendered most of the ship's rigging unusable as well." That evening, with the vessel adrift northwest of South Haven, Captain Thompson ordered the main anchor to be lowered.

Early the following morning, a surfman on duty at the South Haven Life Saving Station spotted *Rockaway* and her crew and notified the station's captain, John H. McKenzie. Around 6:30 a.m., the station's lifeboat was launched and headed northwest for *Rockaway*. "Arriving at the vessel we found the crew in pitiable condition," wrote McKenzie in his report. "The Mate, the Captain's son, had his hand badly frozen . . . and could not help himself at all. The Captain Ole Thompson and one of the crew could scarcely move . . . and it was all we could do to keep those three awake on the passage home." At the life-saving station, the crew ate a warm breakfast, and the mate was attended by a local physician.

On November 19, the steam-tug *L. S. Paine*, the schooner *Daisy*, and the life-saving crew sailed out to *Rockaway*, planning to take her in tow. Unfortunately, arriving on the scene, only the scow's fore-topmast was visible. She had sunk in seventy feet of water.

Rockaway's career and demise were typical of vessels serving in the Great Lakes schooner trade. Storms, shoals, and fire doomed scores of schooners. Between 1878 and 1898, over six thousand vessels wrecked on the lakes, with approximately one thousand total losses.

Almost a century later, as the archaeological work progressed, a picture of what *Rockaway* had looked like began to emerge. "Although some cost-cutting measures were taken in the *Rockaway*'s construction, these measures were not typical of the compromise so often attributed to the building of scows," said Pott. "In fact, there was no strong evidence to indicate that economy of build was a significant influence in the choice of this vessel's design. Although classified as a scow-schooner,

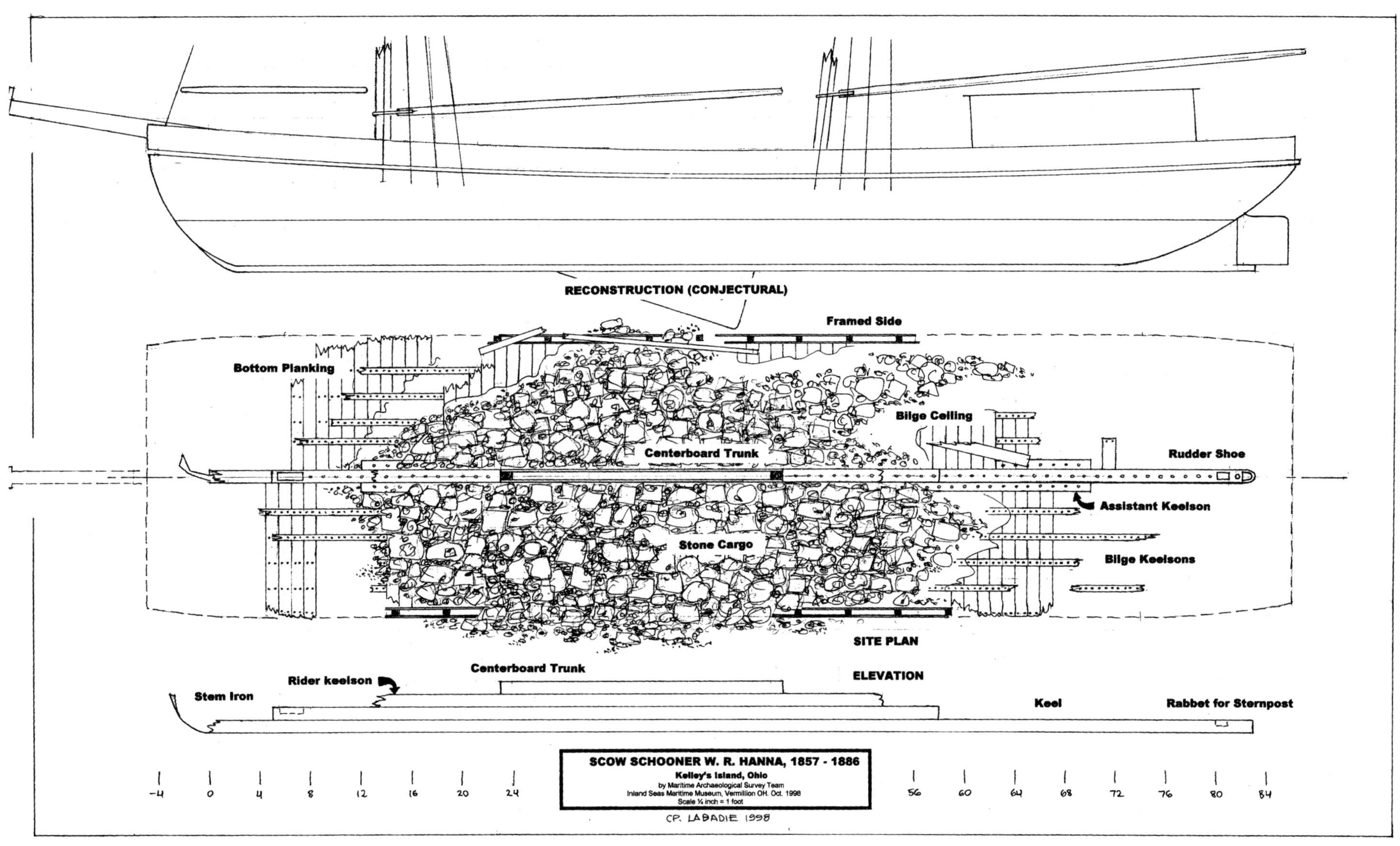

The scow-schooner *W. R. Hanna*, carrying a cargo of stones, was wrecked off Kelley's Island in Lake Erie in 1886. This archaeological site plan, drawn by Michigan maritime historian C. Patrick Labadie in 1998, illustrated the vessel's position on the lake's bottom.

COURTESY OF THUNDER BAY NATIONAL MARINE SANCTUARY, C. PATRICK LABADIE COLLECTION

Rockaway was built of relatively complex form, and with materials characterized as 'first class' by the 1866 Lake Underwriters Rules."

"Our study of the *Rockaway* clearly indicates that the Great Lakes scow schooner was a vessel of more varied design and construction than historical characterizations suggest, and that the desire for a certain quality and versatility of function was at least as influential in the minds of the vessel's builders and owners as cost of construction. Instead, the [ship's] architectural characteristics indicate a sophisticated level of knowledge, skill, and innovation on the part of its designers and builders."

While most scow-schooners had a distinctive, box-like hull, *Rockaway* had a spoon bow integrated with her bottom, shaped with a gentle, multifaceted deadrise, somewhere between hard-chined and flat-bottomed construction. The multi-chined hull proved more sea kindly. This design also produced a ship whose topsides would be less likely to snag pilings or wharf structures during loading and unloading.

CANAL SCHOONERS

Canal schooners—known as "canallers"—were primarily developed to navigate the Welland Canal (near Niagara Falls, New York). They opened up trade via the St. Lawrence River and were most commonly seen on Lake Ontario and Lake Huron. "While as much curvature as possible was built into the hulls for purposes of speed, efforts were made to build boxy hulls that could maximize cargo-carrying capacity with the efficiency of sail," said Ken Pott. Canal schooners were designed to carry as much cargo as possible, given the canal's restrictions on size. Until the late 1870s, canal vessels could not exceed an LOA of 142'5" and a beam of 26'3" and were towed through the canal by teams of horses or oxen.

"The canallers were probably the most standardized sailing craft ever employed on the Lakes," said maritime historian Patrick Labadie. "I think there were at least 600 of them, and probably more, between 1850 and 1880." These were narrow, wall-sided vessels, with straight stems and a flat transom. They carried short, stubby bowsprits, which

The canal schooner *Cornelia B. Windiate* departing Milwaukee, 1875, by Robert McGreevy (watercolor 20 × 30 inches, courtesy of Thunder Bay National Marine Sanctuary).
© ROBERT MCGREEVY

The canal schooner *Henry Fitzhugh*, seen resting in drydock, was launched in Oswego, New York, in 1886. After decades of sailing the Great Lakes, she was relegated to work as a schooner-barge until the 1920s. COURTESY OF THUNDER BAY NATIONAL MARINE SANCTUARY, C. PATRICK LABADIE COLLECTION

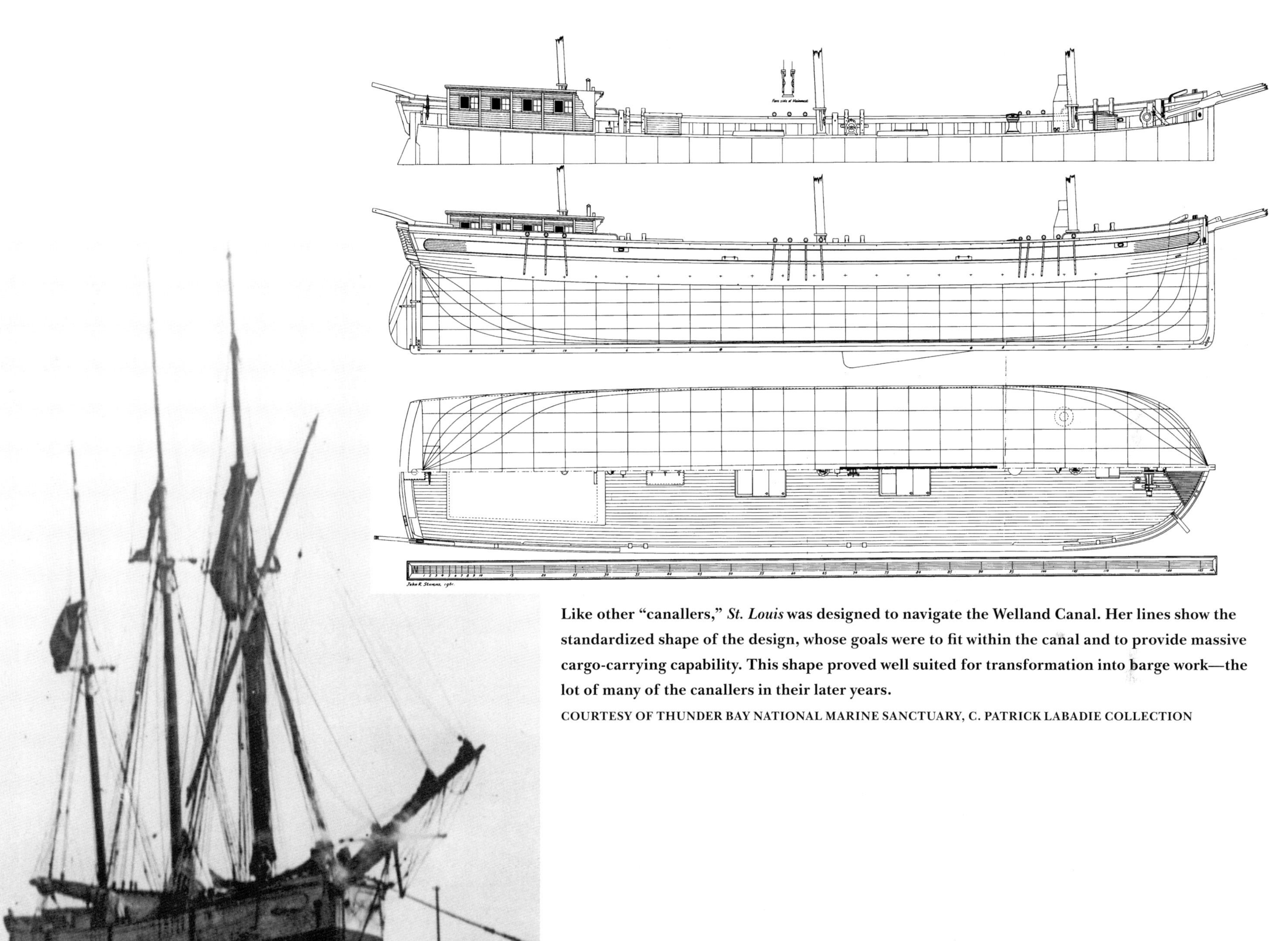

Like other "canallers," *St. Louis* was designed to navigate the Welland Canal. Her lines show the standardized shape of the design, whose goals were to fit within the canal and to provide massive cargo-carrying capability. This shape proved well suited for transformation into barge work—the lot of many of the canallers in their later years.

COURTESY OF THUNDER BAY NATIONAL MARINE SANCTUARY, C. PATRICK LABADIE COLLECTION

were hinged to be rotated upwards while passing through the locks, allowing the greatest possible hull length. Their narrow, flat-bottom design made them hard to handle in heavy weather.

One prominent canaller was *St. Louis*, built in 1877 by Louis Shickluna at St. Catherines, Ontario, Canada. With an LOA of 127'8", a 26'2" beam, and drawing 11'11", she was a sizable vessel in her class. During her early years on the Lakes, *St. Louis* carried grain between Duluth, Minnesota, and Kingston, Ontario. By the late 1880s, the vessel had been converted to a tow barge, still carrying grain but tethered behind a steam barge, often with one or more similar tow barges or "consorts." Through the 1890s, the steamer *L. S. Shickluna* regularly towed *St. Louis*. In September 1897, both vessels, bound from Port Arthur, Ontario, to Kingston with a load of grain, were driven hard aground near Fish Point, four miles south of Oscoda, Michigan, on Lake Huron. *Shickluna* was soon hauled free by the tug *Thompson*, but *St. Louis* wasn't pulled to deep water until October, when she was towed to Port Huron, Michigan, for repairs before being returned to service. Her career ended in 1911 when she was declared unfit and abandoned at Kingston. Later, in 1926, she was sunk in Lake Ontario off Nine Mile Point. Such was the stormy life of these robust vessels.

THE MOSQUITO FLEET

A group of smaller sailing craft, schooners or sloops under 100' in length, were part of the so-called mosquito fleet and were considered pests by the captains of larger vessels. These diminutive, short-haul vessels were frequently built by their owner-skippers on the banks of rivers all around the Great Lakes, using local materials. They were built with rougher finishes and were considerably less comfortable than the larger vessels on the Lakes. These unpretentious boats were the short-haul truckers of their time, serving maritime communities from Lake Ontario to Lake Superior. While the large schooners—some stretching over 200' in length and owned by lumber, mining, or manufacturing companies—sailed throughout the Lakes, the mosquito craft generally stayed close to their home ports.

On Lake Michigan, maritime communities had been established along the shores of Wisconsin,

The *Lettie May*—47' LOA, with a 14' beam and 7' depth—was typical of the small schooners plying the Great Lakes. Built at Fort Howard (Green Bay) in 1874, she sailed in the mosquito fleet on Lake Michigan until she was wrecked on October 4, 1905. COURTESY OF THUNDER BAY NATIONAL MARINE SANCTUARY, C. PATRICK LABADIE COLLECTION

Illinois, Indiana, and Michigan, with Chicago being a major port and a hub for goods moving west via the railroad and river systems. The small vessels, many of them scows, linked these communities and were able to conduct trade, providing local products in exchange for goods they could not produce themselves. A long passage for short haulers would have been a few hundred miles, sailing along the shoreline from town to town or crossing Lake Michigan to carry on trade.

When the weather was not an obstacle, and the supply and demand of products were healthy, short haulers made money. But in the winter months, and during periods of inclement weather, the small craft, with a few exceptions, sat at anchor, and sailors found work ashore. The handful who chose to sail through the winter risked having their vessels frozen in ice or foundering on a lee shore in a storm. Mosquitoes may have been an annoyance to the skippers of the big vessels, but these little ships left a large and memorable legacy on the Lakes. At times, they were called upon to respond to emergencies as well as carrying goods.

On Sunday evening, October 8, 1871, a raging firestorm swept across the Upper Midwest, from Minnesota to Michigan, reducing communities and some of their inhabitants to ashes, and laying waste to forests and farmland. This was the same night that the Great Chicago Fire killed three hundred people and destroyed over three square miles in the city's center. The Great Peshtigo Fire, the deadliest in US history, roared through 1.2 million acres in northeastern Wisconsin, driven by 100-mile-per-hour winds, consuming several towns and killing from fifteen hundred to twenty-five hundred people. Across Lake Michigan, three massive blazes flared up at Holland, Port Huron, and Manistee, Michigan. The Great Michigan Fire burned 2.5 million acres of primary forest land, killing more than five hundred people and possibly hundreds more. The conflagrations' exact causes remain a mystery, but the rain hadn't fallen in many places for months. The landscape was tinder-dry, a danger needing only a spark to set it alight and winds to fan the flames. Dry vegetation and logging debris called "slash" fueled the fires. In some areas, small land-clearing fires merged, creating massive walls of flames driven by gale-force winds.

Survivors faced even more suffering the following winter, one of the worst recorded up to that time. Fluctuating winds spared many shoreline communities in Wisconsin, but several inland towns and villages were not so lucky. Unlike major cities like Chicago or Green Bay, small maritime communities without rail service were cut off from the outside world. Short-haul schooners were their only source for supplies critical to surviving the harsh winter. Despite the risks, this small fleet and their brave crews sailed through the winter, with ice-covered sails and rigging, ice flows in the lake, and heavy seas. When the bitter cold abated and spring arrived in 1872, the mosquito schooners assisted rebuilding efforts for Chicago and other communities devastated by the fires, hauling lumber from the northern reaches of Michigan and Wisconsin, and other construction materials, like stone and shingles. That summer, Lake Michigan was a superhighway packed with small, white-winged vessels at work.

CAPTAIN GEORGE JEPSON

On October 8, 1884, the small, two-masted schooner *Mamie Jepson* drove into towering seas on Lake Michigan, shrouded in middle-watch darkness, with only a staysail aloft. Gale-force winds tore through her rigging as green water swept over the decks. The autumn storm, common on the Great Lakes, blew up suddenly from the northeast after midnight, threatening all vessels at large on the lake. By daylight, Captain George Jepson, my great-grandfather, safely guided the battered schooner between the piers at Racine, Wisconsin, and into the Root River, with her cargo, more than likely produce or shingles. Reporting on the storm, the *Chicago Tribune* said, "The small schr [*sic*] *Mamie Jepson* narrowly escaped being wrecked, and came in with her bow stove in." A few miles from the *Mamie Jepson*, the Goodrich passenger steamer *Muskegon*, bound for Milwaukee, "experienced a rough time five miles north of [Racine]," according to the *Tribune*. "The heavy seas crushed in thirty feet of the upper works of her starboard bow. . . ." Such was the threat that late-season shipping posed on Lake Michigan.

———◇◇◇◇◇———

After the Great Fires in 1871, Captain Jepson, then residing in Chicago, was sailing in the schooner trade on Lake Michigan. By 1880, he captained his own vessel, the 67', twenty-one-ton *Mamie Jepson*, built and based in Manistee, Michigan, and named for his wife.

Captain George Jepson, shown in this circa 1880s studio portrait in Manistee, Michigan, was like most schooner masters on Lake Michigan, a businessman first and a sailor second.

The small schooner hauled lumber, shingles, and seasonal produce (apples, peaches, and vegetables) to communities along Michigan's western shore and across the lake to Chicago and Wisconsin ports.

Although the shipping season began early in the spring and lasted until November, the mosquito schooners, usually owned and sailed by their captains, were known to risk sailing as soon as the ice melted in the spring and continued well into the winter months, often at their own peril. Captain Jepson was no exception.

On January 4, 1882, *The Weekly Wisconsin* reported: "The schooner Mamie Jepson, bound for [Manistee], went on the beach at Hamilton, just south of Big Point au Sable, at 2 o'clock Saturday morning." According to the same article, the Point au Sable life-saving crew told Captain Jepson "that they had found the wreck of the [schooner] *Orphan Boy* on the beach about fifteen miles south of here, and also had found one body. The wreck is reported to be nearly cut in two, as though the schooner had a collision."

The Daily Inter Ocean, a Chicago-based newspaper, reported on April 22, 1884: "A heavy northeast gale has prevailed [at Manitowoc, Wisconsin] since yesterday morning." The *Mamie Jepson* was listed as one of several vessels seeking shelter. Similar news about vessels was regularly transmitted by telegraph throughout the sailing season to ports around the Great Lakes and published in local newspapers.

On January 2, 1887, *Mamie Jepson*, bound for Manistee along the Michigan coast, "with a cargo of barreled apples and a crew of two men, went ashore a

There are no known photographs of the schooner *Mamie Jepson*. However, the schooner *Active*—68' LOA, with a 17' beam and 5' depth—had lines similar to those of *Mamie Jepson*. *Active* was built in Sheboygan, Wisconsin, in 1869 in the Olsen Brothers shipyard. This photo appears to show the vessel beached near the Charlevoix, Michigan, South Pier Lighthouse on Lake Michigan.

COURTESY OF THUNDER BAY NATIONAL MARINE SANCTUARY, C. PATRICK LABADIE COLLECTION

mile and a quarter south of the Grand Point au Sable Station," according to the annual report of the United States Life Saving Service. "The night was dark and misty and the vessel was standing up the coast under a light southeasterly breeze. Near daylight the keeper was roused by the captain of the stranded craft to request assistance. The regular life-saving force being off duty for the winter a volunteer crew was mustered, and, with lines, tackles, and an anchor, repaired as soon as possible to the scene. . . ." Surfmen off-loaded the cargo but failed to heave the vessel off the beach. The tug *John D. Dewar* arrived a day later and pulled the schooner free, tearing away her windlass. Late that evening, the steamer *Onekama* towed her to Manistee,

barely escaping a gale and heavy seas that swept across the lake from the northwest.

The small schooners like *Mamie Jepson* played a critical role in developing and supplying the Lake Michigan region with necessary goods well into the 1880s, sailing against the weather's whims. Delivering cargoes to ports on both sides of the lake often meant being confined to the river or harbors until winds turned favorable. Consequently, maritime businessmen operating short-haul schooners like Captain Jepson depended on timely passages to turn profits, particularly when delivering perishable produce. After nearly a decade in the schooner trade, Captain Jepson transitioned to steamers in the late 1880s.

THE LAST COMMERCIAL SCHOONERS

The three-masted schooner *Our Son*—182'1" LOA, with a 35'1" beam, and a 13' depth—sailed the Great Lakes for fifty-five years when most wooden vessels were fortunate to last much beyond fifteen years unless cared for conscientiously. Built in 1874 at the Lyon, Wallace & Garon shipyard at Black River, Ohio, the vessel's name laid bare Captain Harry Kelley's grief after his eldest child died. "The name also reflected the commitment of Kelley and his wife to both commemorate their loss and to work through their grief to build a better future for the rest of their family," wrote Theodore J. Karamanski in his book *Schooner Passage: Sailing Ships and the Lake Michigan Frontier.* "For them the ship was both an end and a beginning."

Initially built for the ore and grain trade, *Our Son* passed through several owners during her notable career. She was a glorious sight at her peak, carrying more sail than any other ship on the Great Lakes. By 1901, she was listed as a schooner barge, towed behind steam-powered vessels, but in 1923,

Our Son as she appeared in her later years. **COURTESY OF THUNDER BAY NATIONAL MARINE SANCTUARY, C. PATRICK LABADIE COLLECTION**

she was re-rigged for sail in the pulpwood trade. *Our Son* foundered off Ludington, Michigan, on September 26, 1930. She had blown across the lake from the Wisconsin shore in a gale. The freighter *William Nelson* rescued her seven-man crew, but within an hour, the vessel slipped beneath the waves, ending a career spanning more than fifty years (see sidebar). She was one of the last two commercial sailing ships on the Great Lakes, only succeeded by the *J. T. Wing* (ex-*Charles F. Gordon*, ex-*J. O. Webster,* and ex-*Oliver H. Perry*).

The Great Lakes schooners, large and small, are now gone, either broken up and burned, resting in the depths of the Great Lakes, or their bleached bones buried under the shifting sands along shorelines. Only a few replica schooners sail the Great Lakes—well over a century after their forebearers first tasted the sweetwater seas.

AN ERA ENDS
The Sheboygan Press
(Sheboygan, Wisconsin)
September 27, 1930
By Associated Press

A glamorous chapter of sail-spread commerce on the Great Lakes was ended today.

The two-master [*sic*], *Our Son*, last of a type that once dappled northern waters disappeared amid crashing waves of a Lake Michigan storm off here after her crew of seven was taken aboard the freighter *William Nelson*.

Built in 1875, the *Our Son* bent its masts before many a storm on the inland seas only to meet disaster during the first of the season's lake storms yesterday. Her captain, Fred Nelson, for fifty-five years answering the lure of smacking canvas on the lakes, stood aboard the *William Nelson* and saw his ship disappear. But his boat fought to the last. And when abandoned, the *Our Son* had her canvas cut. To leave her with sails hopefully spread would have been a sacrilege, Captain Nelson argued.

Capt. C. H. Mohr of the *William Nelson* sighted the *Our Son* flying distress signals. He risked his ship to save the schooner's crew. Seas pounded high and rescue work even with

Freighter *William Nelson*. COURTESY OF THUNDER BAY NATIONAL MARINE SANCTUARY, C. PATRICK LABADIE COLLECTION

newfangled ships was difficult. Within hailing distance, he shouted to the *Our Son* to head into the wind and prepare to leave ship. With a last effort, the schooner responded. The *William Nelson* shoved her bow alongside and—but it's best told in the words of Captain Mohr in a special radio to the Associated Press via WSK, the C. Reiss Coal company station here.

Captain's Message

In part, Captain Mohr's radio follows:

"We sighted the schooner, *Our Son* at 3:30 p.m., northeast of Sheboygan. She was flying distress signals. We turned the William Nelson about and circled her. When in hailing distance, we asked the crew of the schooner to head into the wind so the *William Nelson* would come alongside. We brought the bow of the Nelson against *Our Son*, battling tremendous seas.

"With the assistance of the crew of the *William Nelson*, the men from the schooner were taken aboard without the aid of life boats, although all life-saving gear had been prepared for use. The *William Nelson* and the entire crew of the *Our Son* is proceeding to Milwaukee.

"As the *William Nelson* approached, the crew of the schooner cut all sails, after the rescue, we watched the *Our Son* for more than 45 minutes. Then she disappeared, believed capsized or sunk."

It was learned here today that the *William Nelson*, with the crew of the *Our Son*, was heading for Chicago, rather than stopping at Milwaukee, as first planned.

As the mid-1860s approached and the American Civil War neared an end, the Great Lakes fleet consisted of nearly two thousand sailing vessels—mostly schooners—and about three hundred general cargo and "propeller" steamers (see Chapter 2). In 1857, a sudden economic downturn caused panic to sweep across America, idling much of the steamer fleet. J. S. Noyes, a ship owner from Buffalo, New York, began converting passenger steamers into barges so forest products could be towed from port to port. Some idle steamers were stripped and made into what became known as "steam barges" (see Chapter 3). This proved to be a profitable as well as efficient means of moving bulk cargoes.

The steam-barge *Colin Campbell* carries a cargo of railroad ties, circa 1895.

The success of these steam barges inspired a Cleveland builder to construct an even larger, double-decked steamer in 1869, designed to carry grain and iron ore below decks. "This was the first 'bulk freighter,' predecessor for the huge Lakers of the later 19th and the 20th century," said Labadie. "Introduction of the bulk freighters was a death-knell for schooners. After 1880, virtually no more full-rigged [topsail] schooners were constructed, and most of the existing schooners ended up as tow-barges." Schooners converted to barges had their topmasts and bowsprits removed, allowing for sails to be rigged for maneuvering in an emergency, or for stability.

Another incentive for converting large schooners to barges occurred in the 1880s when the seamen's union enforced a higher pay rate for members who worked aboard sailing vessels. Smaller schooners, which were not unionized, continued into the 1920s, carrying coal and lumber until their aging timbers weakened, or until replacing aging sails and rigging was no longer economical.

The converted schooners faced increased hazards while towing behind steamers, besides those encountered in adverse conditions on the Lakes. An article in the August 21, 1898, *Detroit Free Press* reported: "The schooner *Alert* in tow of the steamer *I. Watson Stephenson* was sunk in the Sturgeon Bay canal this morning by collision with the steamer towing her. The *Stephenson* went aground after the accident. She now rests on the bottom in the narrows. The *Alert* can be saved. Both boats are laden with lumber from the port of Chicago."

DESIGNER/BUILDER WILLIAM WALLACE BATES

William Wallace Bates was one of the most prominent shipwrights on the Great Lakes during the schooner era. As a young man, Bates began learning his trade under the tutelage of his father, Stephen, in Calais, Maine. By the time he was eighteen, he had designed his first ship. In 1851, at the age of twenty-four, he moved with his wife, Marie, his father, and his father's family to Manitowoc, Wisconsin. Soon after their arrival, he and his father opened Bates & Son Shipyard, and laid the keel for a new schooner, which tied design concepts learned on the East Coast to the needs of Great Lakes mariners.

The new vessel, appropriately named *Challenge*, borrowed elements from the Baltimore Clipper. The rakish-looking schooner was swift, fine-lined, and sharp-bowed, with a pivoted centerboard, and a nearly round bottom. Yet, her shoal draft enabled entry into the notoriously shallow harbors on the Lakes. She was faster and had increased cargo-carrying capacities. The *Challenge* was 85'10" LOA, had a 22'5" beam, and a 6'6½" draft. She was launched on May 5, 1852, and, along with *Clipper City*, a larger craft that Bates launched two years later (100'11" LOA, 27'6" beam, and 7'7" draft), set the standard for Great Lakes schooners.

Bates's clipper-schooners became a sensation among shipbuilders on the Lakes and launched a shipbuilding tradition in Manitowoc that continues today. In addition to their new design concepts, Bates & Son's early success was fueled by the demand for more vessels to carry lumber, availability of good shipbuilding timber, and a local skilled workforce.

Bates-built vessels were known for their speed and increased cargo-carrying capabilities. Legend has it that

William Wallace Bates. PUBLIC DOMAIN

Clipper City, considered the fastest schooner on the Great Lakes, was once timed sailing from Manitowoc to Sheboygan, Wisconsin, in eighty minutes at 18 miles per hour. Bates's clipper-schooners established him as one of the most skillful and forward-thinking shipbuilders on the Great Lakes, with orders from Milwaukee and Chicago, and gave Manitowoc the name "Clipper City."

ABOVE: Howard Chapelle, who took these lines of William Bates's centerboard "Clipper"-type schooner, *Challenge*, noted her as being the first distinctive Great Lakes schooner type. He also remarked on the ease at which she could attain 13 knots.
LEFT: The Great Lakes schooner *Challenge*, moored in Sheboygan (Wisconsin) Harbor, was launched in 1852 at Manitowoc and sailed until she was wrecked in 1910.
COURTESY OF THUNDER BAY NATIONAL MARINE SANCTUARY, C. PATRICK LABADIE COLLECTION.

Great Lakes schooners turned handsome profits for their owners between the 1840s and 1870s. Merchants willingly invested in vessels built by shipwrights like Bates, with the finest workmanship and fitted out with the best gear. Many of the Bates-built ships were blessed with long lives, sailing the Lakes for over fifty years, *Challenge*, for example, built in the early 1850s, plied the waters of Lake Michigan until September 5, 1910, when she was blown ashore near Sheboygan, and broken up by heavy seas.

A national depression in the 1850s, followed by the American Civil War, nearly halted shipbuilding in Manitowoc. Still, Bates's reputation procured the company contracts to build two steamers for the Goodrich Steamboat Line. After the Civil War ended, Bates sold the Manitowoc shipyard and moved to Chicago, where he helped develop rules for designing and constructing Great Lakes vessels. In 1874, Bates played a prominent role in a meeting of Great Lakes shipbuilders. This meeting resulted in creating a manual called "Rules of Shipbuilding," which presented scientific principles as they applied to ship design. He died in 1911.

SWEETWATER SAILORS

Great Lakes schooner sailors often had no formal qualifications, training, or experience. Instead, they learned by sailing before the mast. On the short-haul vessels, ownership frequently dictated who was in command, as there were no government regulations at the time.

A large number of foreign-born sailors were on the Great Lakes during the schooner era. This group included many Norwegians born into maritime families who sailed the oceans for years before settling on the Great Lakes.

Conditions aboard schooners were also more favorable for Great Lakes crews than their oceangoing counterparts. The food was excellent and fresh. Everyone, including the captain, ate together as equals until the meal ended.

In addition to better pay than the seafaring life on the oceans could offer, a principal attraction was being able to spend more time with their families, frequently returning between voyages to enjoy home life.

The steamer *New Orleans*, shown off Thunder Bay Island, 1849 (oil on canvas 15 × 25 inches, courtesy of the Thunder Bay Marine Sanctuary). The vessel was built on the hull of the steamer *Vermillion*, which burned to the waterline at Huron, Ohio, on November 7, 1842. The hull was towed to Detroit, where *New Orleans* was built in 1844 by B. Goodsell. The three-decked steamer had a 185'4" LOA, with a 26'6" beam and a 12'10" draft. © ROBERT MCGREEVY

Passenger Steamers

THE WAY WEST

A whistle pierced the mid-afternoon air, smoke belched from tall twin funnels, and great paddles churned the water, sending a shudder through the single-deck wooden passenger steamer *Constitution* at Sandusky, Ohio. Bound for Buffalo, New York, in late April 1842, the side-wheeler—149' length on deck (LOD), with a 28'1" beam and 11'10" depth—was a spectacle as she departed the sleepy hamlet along the southern shore of Lake Erie.

Among the voyagers were English novelist Charles Dickens and his wife, Kate, who had arrived in Sandusky by rail the previous evening (see sidebar on page 44). The Dickens were on a grand tour of the United States and Canada, reaching as far west as St. Louis, which the author documented in his memoir, *American Notes for General Circulation.*

In the mid-1830s, Americans looked westward, to the Great Lakes region and beyond to the wilderness in the country's heartland. Land speculators hoped to capitalize on virgin lands around the Lakes, while New Englanders and immigrants sought fresh starts. Traveling by water was the easiest way. Narrow canal boats pulled by teams of horses and mules, packed with families and household goods, passed through the "Grand Erie" and feeder canals to Buffalo. The Lakes began at Buffalo for immigrant Americans. Europeans, Scandinavians, the Irish, and people from Baltic and Slavic countries came by the hundreds of thousands.

By the early 1840s, New Englanders and immigrants seeking a fresh start as America expanded westward favored passage aboard steamers through the Great Lakes. Overland journeys tested a person's sufferance. Stagecoaches, slung on leather strapping between axles jerked along over crude highways or pikes, and they were primitive at best. So, it's little wonder that Dickens booked steamer berths for himself and Kate. *Constitution*, launched in 1837 at Conneaut, Ohio, steamed over the horizon, portending the future of travel on the Great Lakes.

Commerce swiftly escalated along the Lower Great Lakes—Ontario and Erie through the St. Clair River to lower Huron—as settlers and land-hungry speculators swarmed into new settlements. As a result, the demand to transport passengers, supplies, and commodities easily exceeded available shipping. In 1836, there were forty-five steamboats on the Lakes. The first steamer to Detroit that year was the *United States* carrying seven hundred passengers. By the end of the sailing season, nearly a hundred vessels docked there.

Side-wheel and propeller steamers were fundamental to westward expansion. They reached their zenith on the Great Lakes before railroad lines connected far-flung waterfront settlements in the states of New York, Pennsylvania, Ohio, Michigan, Indiana, Illinois, the Wisconsin Territory that eventually became the states of Wisconsin and Minnesota, and Ontario, Canada. By the early 1850s, railroads were beginning to augment overland service with their own steamboat subsidiaries to carry passengers and freight between railheads, which broadened their reach well into middle America and Canada. This combination service gave steamers a new purpose, extending the useful lives of many into the early 1900s.

Other steamers, designed primarily for the excursion trade, were in use on smaller inland lakes and rivers during this period. Steamboats of the western rivers, another breed entirely, were running at this same time, but the Great Lakes steamers—like those operating along the Eastern coastline—had deeper, heavier displacement hulls with higher freeboard for negotiating rough

The steamer *Walk-in-the-Water* arriving at Detroit, August 1818, by Robert McGreevy (watercolor 10 × 17 inches, private collection). The Indian name pertained to the flailing side wheels, which appeared to be a walking motion. *Walk-in-the-Water* ran primarily between Buffalo and Detroit on Lake Erie. Robert McGreevy's painting was based on the earliest known model of the steamer. However, the artist later determined that she was likely painted white. © ROBERT MCGREEVY

waters. This design difference set them apart from other steamer types and proved crucial to the development of the Midwest.

EARLY SIDE-WHEEL STEAMERS

The first Great Lakes steamers, which went into operation after the War of 1812, were schooner-rigged for emergency and auxiliary power, with hulls shaped like sailing ships, paddle wheels located amidships, and a single smokestack between them. *Frontenac*—170' length on deck, with a 32' beam and 11' depth—was built near Kingston, Ontario, and went into service in 1817. *Ontario*—112' LOD, 28' in the beam, with an 8'3" depth—was built at Sackets Harbor, New York, and began operating a few days before *Frontenac*. These two ships led the way for steam navigation on the Great Lakes.

Walk-in-the-Water, similar in design to *Frontenac* and *Ontario,* was the first steamboat constructed for use above Niagara Falls. Built by New York shipwright Noah Brown, this steamer measured 135' LOD, with a 32' beam and an 8'6" depth. Launched at Black Rock (Buffalo) on August 23,

1818, she was powered by a "square" (or A-frame) 60-horsepower (hp), condensing, low-pressure, vertical crosshead engine, and carried two masts with a stack between her 15'-diameter paddle wheels. She was steered from the stern. Later steamers had their wheelhouses located forward, near the bow. Her maiden voyage was from Buffalo to Detroit, a passage of thirty-six to forty hours in clear weather that consumed thirty-six to forty cords of wood.

Almost three years after running exclusively on Lake Erie, *Walk-in-the-Water* inaugurated inter-lake navigation. On July 31, 1821, she left Detroit bound for Green Bay, Wisconsin, carrying two hundred passengers, including members of an expedition formed by Michigan territorial governor Lewis Cass to explore the southern shore of Lake Superior and the upper Mississippi region. Passing from Lake Huron through the Straits of Mackinac, she became the first steamboat to operate on Lake Michigan, just as she previously had been on Lake Erie and Lake Huron. Interestingly, four years would elapse before another steamer would return to Lake Michigan.

A PROPHETIC NOTICE
BUFFALO JOURNAL, OCTOBER 23, 1821

Pursuant to a resolution of the Board of Directors of the Lake Erie Steam-Boat Company, public notice is hereby given that all goods, wares and merchandise, furniture, plate, jewels and specie which may be shipped or transported on board the Steam-Boat *Walk-in-the-Water*, belonging to the said Company, shall be at risk of the respective or shippers thereof, and that the said Company, or the Stockholders thereof, will not pay, nor hold themselves, either individually or as a company, responsible or liable for any loss or damage which may happen in the shipment, transportation or delivery of either of the articles aforesaid; and that the Captain of the Steam-Boat is to receive no freight but upon the conditions in this resolution.

Huron (165' LOA, 23'7" beam, and 9'5" depth) was built in 1852 by Samuel and Eber Ward at Newport (Marine City), Michigan, at a cost of $30,000. Her size was typical of the early Lake Michigan side-wheel paddle steamers. The Wards ran *Huron* between Detroit and Saginaw and Bay City, Michigan, until 1855, when she was sold to another operator. COURTESY OF THUNDER BAY NATIONAL MARINE SANCTUARY, C. PATRICK LABADIE COLLECTION

On October 31, 1821, *Walk-in-the-Water* ran into gale-force winds and driving rain after leaving Buffalo en route to Detroit. Early the following morning, having struggled through the night, she was driven ashore by the wind and broken up near Buffalo. Fortunately, there was no loss of life. Her owners salvaged the engine and other machinery and transferred them to the steamer *Superior* in 1822.

Steam navigation on the Lakes during those early years was perilous. Weather forecasts didn't exist, requiring captains to rely on their instincts. Storms blew up with little warning, and natural harbors were few. Shifting sandbars often blocked channel entrances, while rain, snow, fog, and the smoke from forest fires often impeded visibility. Unmarked boulders and shoals lurked beneath the inaccurately charted surface.

Until lighthouses and navigation buoys were introduced, Great Lakes mariners sailed with great uncertainty. The region's first beacon was lit in 1818 on Lake Erie near Erie, Pennsylvania. Fort Gratiot Light, erected in 1825 at the entrance to the St. Clair River in Michigan, was the first light on Lake Huron. The first Canadian lighthouse went into service in 1847 at Goderich, Ontario. As traffic on the Lakes increased, so too did the number of aids to navigation.

During the 1830s and 1840s, steamboats rapidly shifted from hulls that resembled sailing ships to new and different hull shapes. In 1833, *Michigan*—145' LOD, with a 29' beam and 11'2" depth—was launched in Detroit by shipbuilder Oliver Newberry. The hull featured a main deck that extended out over the paddle boxes but curved inward forward and aft to meet the bow and stern. The additional width amidships allowed a cabin to be built on the main deck, which became a hallmark of Lakes side-wheelers. Before this breakthrough, most cabins were located below the main deck in the fashion of oceangoing steamers.

Not every new development was successful. With an eye toward improving stability, Newberry unwittingly introduced a new wrinkle in *Michigan*, installing two 80-hp vertical beam engines independently connected to 28'-diameter paddle

At 145' LOA, *Michigan* was the largest steamer on the Great Lakes when she was launched in 1833. She was powered by twin vertical beam engines, whose walking beams are visible between the paddle boxes in this illustration by Samuel Ward Stanton. *Michigan* was abandoned and broken up near Buffalo, New York, in 1841. AUTHOR'S COLLECTION

wheels. Speeds up to 15 mph were possible in calm waters, but in heavier seas, the independent power of each wheel accentuated the boat's propensity to roll from side to side, one wheel rising awkwardly out of the water and spinning while the other labored underwater, making steering difficult.

Another significant innovation appeared in 1838, with the launch of the clipper-bowed *Great Western*—183' LOD, 34'5" beam, and 13' depth—at Huron, Ohio. Shipwrights fitted her with the first full-length upper-deck cabin—a concept replicated on most steamers that followed. The spaces below the main deck housed the boilers, engine, firewood, and freight. The ladies' cabin and staterooms were aft on the main deck, while the saloon, dining room, and bar were on the hurricane or top deck. *Great Western* regularly ran from Buffalo to Chicago as one of the Great Lakes' finest steamers.

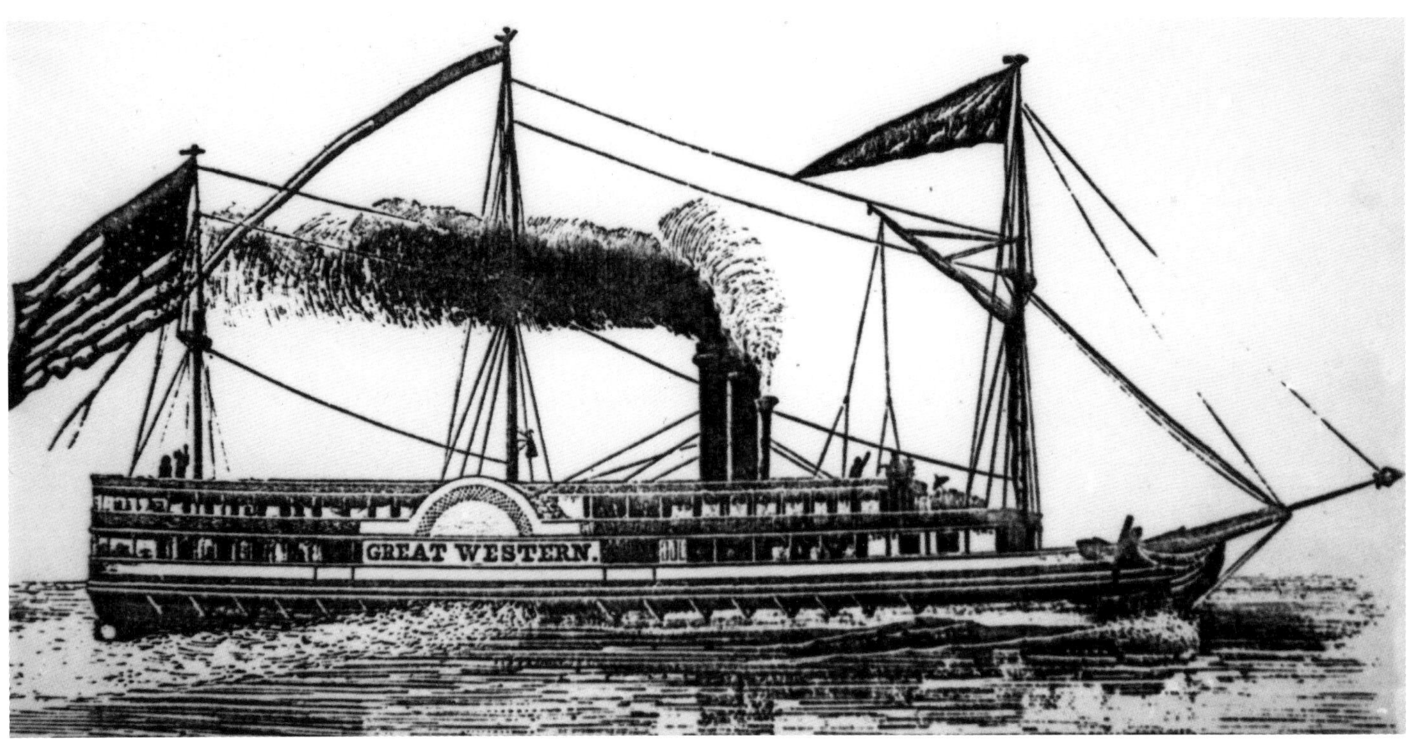

The *Great Western* was a regular on the Buffalo-to-Chicago route between 1838 and the early 1850s. Despite two fires in 1839 and collisions in 1843, 1844, and 1852, the double-decked vessel survived the ruggedest elements of the Great Lakes until 1855, when she was dismantled. COURTESY OF THUNDER BAY NATIONAL MARINE SANCTUARY, C. PATRICK LABADIE COLLECTION

PALACE STEAMERS

By the 1840s, economic pressures had created keen competition among steamboat owners for a greater share of the passenger trade. This motivated designers and shipbuilders to create even larger vessels. The result was the so-called palace steamers, which were larger, faster, and more lavishly appointed than their predecessors. *Empire*—253'6" LOD, with a 32'8½" beam and 14'2" depth—was the first of these enormous boats. Built in Cleveland by shipwright George W. Jones, she was launched on June 1, 1844. The palace steamer era would be short-lived, however, lasting only until the economic Panic of 1857, but by then, at least twenty-five of these magnificent vessels had been built.

Among the exquisite accoutrements on palace steamers, passengers enjoyed luxurious cabins with arched ceilings lit by skylights and stained glass domes by day and by dazzling chandeliers in the evenings. Paneled passenger spaces were painted white and trimmed with gilded moldings that set off the fine upholstered furniture and plush carpets. The last of the breed was *City of Buffalo*—331' LOD, 40' beam, and 15'7" depth—launched in 1857 in Buffalo. She had only operated a month on Lake Erie before the financial panic forced her out of service for nearly two years.

The great size of these vessels was made possible by iron fastenings and diagonal strapping and the development of large, arch-shaped hogging trusses that resembled today's suspension bridges and longitudinally stiffened the long and limber hulls. Athwartships timbers in the holds supported the heavy engines and boilers. Tall A-frames were fastened to the timbers to support and stabilize the exposed walking beam that sat above the hurricane decks and drove the monstrous paddle wheels.

Interest in Gothic architectural style was back in vogue during the palace steamer era, and shipwrights adapted and incorporated fine architectural details into wheelhouse designs. Gilded spheres or eagles graced the crowns of fancy domes, and pilothouse windows came in various shapes to provide an eye-pleasing flourish and a clear view for the helmsman.

"A FINER CRAFT NE'ER FLOATED ON OUR INLAND SEAS" *MILWAUKEE COMMERCIAL HERALD*, OCTOBER 29-31, 1844

A correspondent for the Milwaukee Commercial Herald, who signed his work as "K," reported from aboard the palace steamer Empire, *bound from Buffalo to Chicago during the vessel's final run of the season.*

Port Sarnia, Canada West, October 29, 1844
To relieve the dull monotony of a Lake steamer in a wind-bound duress, I have adopted the pastime of apprising you of our "whereabouts," and detailing in minutiae the various incidents that go to enliven what would otherwise be a somewhat irksome detention in an equinoctial gale.

The steamer *Empire*—and a finer craft ne'er floated on our inland seas—with a spaciousness that scarcely knows dimensions—with accommodations that cannot be surpassed by the best city hotels—with a commander the very prince of good fellows, affable, gentlemanly, and courteous to all—with a crew undaunted in storm and peril, and veteran service—the *Empire*, I repeat, the pride and glory of our lakes—*the Empire*, for there is none like her—left Buffalo on the evening of Friday, the 26th, with 400 tons of merchandise, and 600 passengers, on her last trip for the season to Chicago.

Clouds lay piled up in grandeur over Niagara. And the far off West was glowing with a crimson sunset, as we left the crowded wharves of Buffalo, and swept out on the broad bosom of Erie . . . After making short stoppages at Cleveland and Detroit, the *Empire* passed St. Clair river on Monday morning, and stood up into Lake Huron. We had proceeded some twenty-five miles when a gale, which was noticed to commence blowing early in the morning, had increased to such fury that it was deemed necessary to return to the St. Clair, and await until it subsided. Accordingly, the order to "about ship" was obeyed and we ran down into the river, and for better security against the violence of the gale, hauled up to the wharf on the British shore, at the little village of Port Sarnia. The gale increased in fury, accompanied with hail, rain, and snow.

Lake Michigan, off Manitou, Thursday night, October 31, 1844
Once more upon the waters! The broad sweeping waves of Lake Michigan are around and above us, heaving and rocking the noble *Empire* and her countless hosts with a sailor's lullaby, into the gentle slumbers! We left Port Sarnia on Wednesday noon. The storm had mostly subsided, and the wind suddenly changing, the heavy sea had almost entirely gone down, when we stood up once more on Lake Huron. After making short stoppages at Presque Isle and Mackinaw, we had a pleasant run through the Straits, and are now passing North Manitou [Island] at a rapid progress of fourteen miles per hour, on our home-bound trip to Milwaukee.

The trip, notwithstanding unavoidable detention, has been very agreeable. The conviction has forced itself upon all the passengers, that had we not returned on Monday morning to the St. Clair, the *Empire*, and her immense freight must have gone to the bottom of Lake Huron! The sea ran tremendously—the wind blew with the fierceness of a hurricane, and no earthly power could have saved us from the horrors of shipwreck.

Empire, the first of the storied palace steamers on the Great Lakes, was launched on June 1, 1844.

Even among the immense palace steamers, collisions, groundings, boiler explosions, fires, and other mishaps were common on the Lakes. For example, on September 1, 1854, the *Cleveland Morning Leader* reported: "The Steamer *Alabama* which left Buffalo August 30, at 4 o'clock in the morning, bound up, sprung a leak when about two miles out, and immediately sunk. Fortunately, she grounded on a bar where the water was not more than 20 feet deep and sank only to her upper deck." At 234'6" LOD, with a 29'2" beam and 12' depth, *Alabama* would have been a serious threat to navigation in those waters until two months later when authorities cleared the wreckage.

When *Lady Elgin* slid down the ways in 1851, she took her place among a fleet of over four hundred side-wheel paddle steamers navigating on the Great Lakes between 1818 and 1924. This rare photograph by Samuel Alschule captures the palace steamer moored to a pier in the Chicago River near LaSalle Street circa 1860 before her last trip. The vessel's massive hogging trusses are made of wood.
COURTESY OF THUNDER BAY NATIONAL MARINE SANCTUARY, C. PATRICK LABADIE COLLECTION

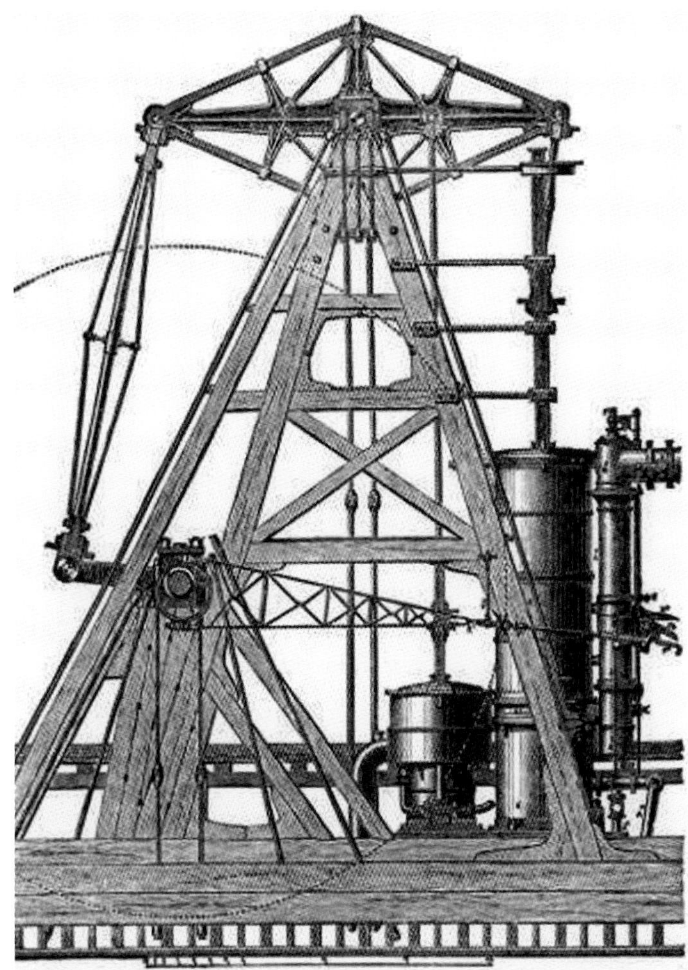

Walking beam engines—also called vertical beam engines—drove many paddle steamers on the Great Lakes during the nineteenth century. The large arc in the illustration phantoms a paddle wheel, which was turned by the wheels' crankshaft.

Lady Elgin—252' LOD, 32'8" beam, and 13' depth—was launched in 1851 at the Bidwell & Banta shipyard in Buffalo. A 350-hp single-cylinder, vertical walking beam engine powered the vessel and drove her twin 32'-diameter wheels. She ran between Buffalo and Lake Michigan ports early in her career. During the Panic of 1857, *Lady Elgin* continued on the Lake Superior and Lake Michigan route with many palace steamers laid up.

She had a hard life, having survived groundings, fire, and collision over her nine years afloat. Then, in the early morning hours of September 7, 1860, on the run from Chicago to Milwaukee in darkness with an excursion party aboard, she was struck by the unlit schooner *Augusta* off Winnetka, Illinois. She went to the bottom of Lake Michigan, taking three hundred souls with her. It was one of the worst disasters ever recorded on Lake Michigan.

Thankfully, most palace steamers did not end in such tragic circumstances. *Mississippi*, among the largest of her class—335' LOD, with a 40' beam and 14' depth—was launched in 1853 at the Francis N. Jones shipyard in Buffalo. She was built for the Buffalo and Sandusky line to run opposite her sister, *St. Lawrence*—326' LOD, with a 40'11" beam and 14'2" depth. In her second year, *Mississippi* was purchased by the Michigan Central Railroad Company (MCR) to operate between Buffalo and Detroit, where westbound passengers connected with MCR rail service across southern Michigan to St. Joseph and, ultimately, again by steamer, to Chicago. Unfortunately, at the end of the decade, the economy, not the Lakes, doomed *Mississippi*.

Although the palace steamer era peaked before the Civil War, many of these surviving behemoths, all built of wood as side-wheelers, continued on the Lakes in the excursion and cross-lake trade but slowly faded away as screw propellers and iron hulls became more dominant.

CHARLES DICKENS AND THE STEAMER *CONSTITUTION*

During Charles Dickens's grand tour of the United States and Canada in 1842, he chronicled his journey in letters to his friend John Forster in England, and later in his book, *American Notes for General Circulation.*

Clamorous clanking and the hiss of steam in the early-evening light signaled the arrival of a railroad locomotive in the quiet Lake Erie port of Sandusky, Ohio, on Saturday, April 23, 1842. Stepping down from a carriage behind the engine, English novelist Charles Dickens—then thirty—and his wife, Kate, hoped to connect with a passenger steamer bound for Buffalo, New York.

After securing overnight accommodations in a small hotel within sight of the lake, Dickens wrote to John Forster that Sandusky is "twenty-four hours journey by steamboat from Buffalo. We found no boat here, nor has there been one, since. We are waiting, with every thing [*sic*] packed up, ready to start on the shortest notice; and are anxiously looking out for smoke in the distance."

Arising on Sunday, April 24, the author wondered whether a boat would appear. "We were taking an early dinner . . . when a steamboat came in sight, and presently touched at the wharf," he wrote in *American Notes*. "As she proved to be on her way to Buffalo, we hurried on board with all speed, and soon left Sandusky far behind us.

There are no known illustrations of the early paddle steamer *Constitution*, which carried English novelist Charles Dickens (inset) on Lake Erie in 1842. The *Thomas Jefferson* was a near twin. AUTHOR'S COLLECTION (BOTH)

"[*Constitution*] was a large vessel of [four] hundred tons, and handsomely fitted up, though with high-pressure engines; which always conveyed that kind of feeling to me, which I should be likely to experience, I think, if I had lodgings on the first-floor of a powder-mill. She was laden with flour, some casks of which commodity were stored upon the deck. The captain coming up to have a little conversation, and to introduce a friend, seated himself astride of one of these barrels, like a Bacchus of private life; and pulling a great clasp-knife out of his pocket, began to 'whittle' it as he talked, by paring thin slices off the edges. And he whittled with such industry and hearty good will, that but for his being called away very soon, it must have disappeared bodily, and left nothing in its place but grist and shavings."

Leaving Sandusky, the side-wheeler steamed along Erie's southern shore. Continuing his chronicle in *American Notes*, Dickens wrote: "After calling at one or two flat places, with low dams stretching out into the lake, whereon were stumpy lighthouses, like windmills without sails, the whole looking like a Dutch vignette, we came at midnight to Cleveland, where we lay all night, and until nine o'clock next morning."

Even in the backwaters of America, Dickens's celebrity proved to be a distraction. "The people poured on board, in crowds, by six on Monday morning, to see me," he lamented in the letter to Forster: "a party of 'gentlemen' actually planted themselves before our little cabin, and stared in at the door and windows while I was washing, and Kate lay in bed. I was so incensed at this. . . ."

After departing Cleveland, *Constitution* steamed to Erie, Pennsylvania, laying over for an hour, and then set a course for Buffalo, arriving the following morning at six o'clock. The Dickenses "went ashore to breakfast; sent to the post-office forthwith; and received—oh! who or what can say with how much pleasure and what unspeakable delight!—our English letters!"

Writing to Forster, Dickens compared the journey with ocean voyages. "It's all very fine talking about Lake Erie," he said, "but it won't do for persons who are liable to sea-sickness. We were all sick. It's almost as bad in that respect as the Atlantic. The waves are very short, and horribly constant."

CAPTAIN FREDERICK MARRYAT IN AMERICA

On April 3, 1837, Captain Frederick Marryat climbed aboard the packet *Quebec* at Spithead off Portsmouth, England. The former British Royal Navy officer, now a celebrated novelist for his sea adventures—including *Peter Simple* and *Midshipman Easy*—was bound for New York. A month later, Marryat stepped ashore in New York. Walking up Broadway, he encountered a populace stunned by a financial panic igniting a depression that would carry into the mid-1840s. The shock caused by the panic was his first opportunity to observe Americans. Over the next two years, he would continue his study, which he described in his six-volume *Diary in America.* By that autumn, he had toured the Great Lakes aboard side-wheel steamers and even a birch-bark canoe. Writing to his mother in October from a Detroit-to-Buffalo steamer on Lake Erie, he summarized his journey:

"I went up the Hudson, crossed to Saratoga, Trenton Falls, Falls of the Mohawk, Oswego River to Lake Ontario; then to Niagara, Buffalo and to Lake Erie—to Detroit; from Detroit to Lake St. Clair and Lake Huron to Mackinan [*sic*], from Mackinan took a bark canoe and crossed the Huron, went up the River St. Clair to the Sault Ste Marie and from thence to Lake Superior."

At Detroit, he boarded the side-wheel steamer *Michigan* for Mackinaw. There he found "a fairy isle floating on the water, which is so pure and transparent that you may see down to almost any depth; and the air above is as pure as the water. . . ."

Captain Frederick Marryat. PUBLIC DOMAIN

Although Marryat spent considerable time aboard steamers, his *Diary in America* primarily emphasized "the vastness and extent of commerce carried on in these inland seas whose coasts are now lined with flourishing towns and cities, and whose waters are ploughed by magnificent steam-boats and hundreds of vessels laden with merchandise. Even the Americans themselves are not fully aware of the rising importance of these Lakes as connected with the West."

Continuing, he observed, "The American government have paid every attention to their inland waters. The harbours, light-houses, piers, etcetera, have all been built at the expense of government, and every precaution has been taken to make the navigation of the Lakes as safe as possible."

Over two years, Marryat cruised through the Great Lakes, visiting towns and cities on both the Canadian and American sides. Additionally, he traveled by canal boat, coach, and rail through New England and New York. A final stop was Washington, DC, in early 1839. Unfortunately, by then, his finances were somewhat depleted, and in June, he returned to quarters at 8 Duke Street, St. James, London.

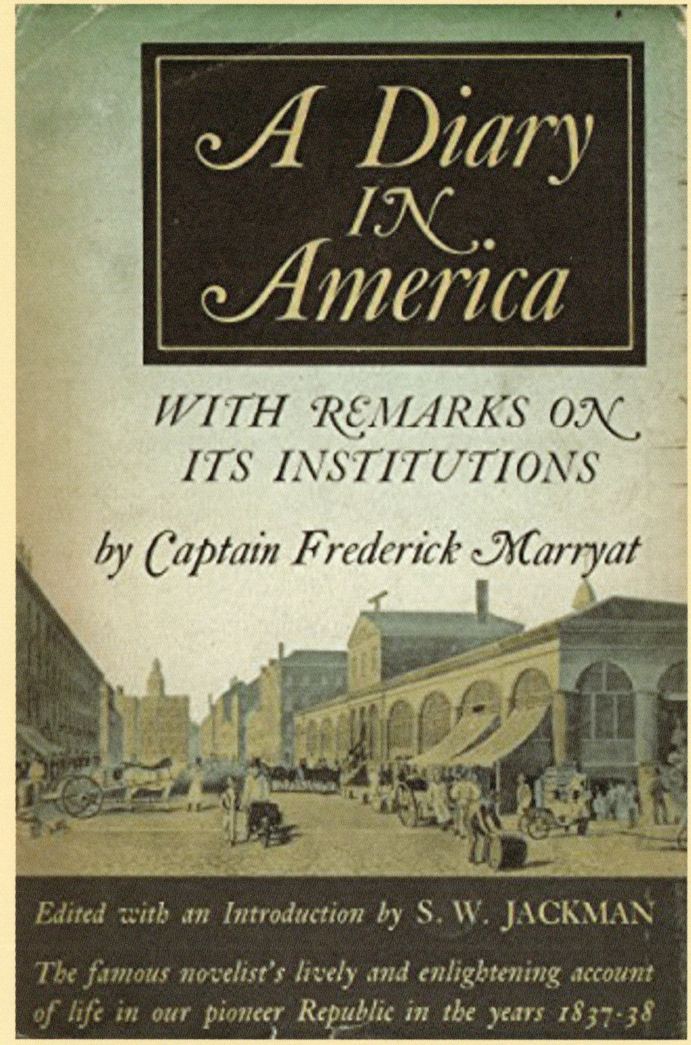

PROPELLER STEAMERS

The screw-propeller-driven steamer—known colloquially as the "propeller"—was first employed in the early 1840s on Lake Ontario. Shipbuilding in the 1800s developed primarily through trial and error. Lessons learned constructing Great Lakes schooners were applied to side-wheelers and propeller-driven steamers.

As canals came into broader use, side-wheel steamers were too wide. Instead, mules towed canal boats on paths along the banks. Reaching the connecting Great Lakes, passengers and goods were transferred to sailing and steam vessels for their westward journeys. During a visit to New York City in late 1840, Captain James Van Cleve examined a propeller invented and patented by John Ericsson. The screw propeller, he believed, would transform shipping on the Great Lakes.

In 1841, the Sylvester Doolittle shipyard at Oswego, New York, launched a screw-driven steamer commissioned by Van Cleve. Christened *Vandalia*, she was 91' LOD, with a 20'2" beam and 8'3" depth. She looked like a traditional sailing ship, with a sloop-rig, cabins on her main deck, and an open-air promenade for passengers.

Two years later, Carrick & Bidwell shipyard at Buffalo launched the first double-deck propeller. *Hercules*—136'3" LOD, 24'10" in the beam, and 8'1" depth—became the prototype hull shape for future propellers. Unencumbered by paddle boxes, the cargo ports of their slab-sided hulls gave direct access to the docks and significantly sped up the loading and unloading operation. In addition, the absence of paddle boxes reduced the beam, making it much easier to transit the Welland Canal between Lake Ontario and Lake Erie.

Beginning with *Hercules*, the typical early Great Lakes propeller vessel carried a single mast and sail for supplemental or emergency power when needed. While propeller steamers were about equal in speed to side-wheelers, averaging 7–8 mph, they burned less wood and thus required fewer stops to replenish cordwood for refueling. The engines and machinery were also much more compact.

In June 1872, shipwright Ira Lafriner built a large propeller of a conventional design and

The propeller *Vandalia in Dry Dock, 1841*, in an imagined scene depicted in a pencil drawing by marine artist Robert McGreevy. © ROBERT MCGREEVY

launched her at Cleveland. *Peerless*—210'4" LOD, with a 31'2" beam and 13' depth—was destined for the Lake Superior trade. She had spacious staterooms and a lengthy upper deck saloon. Freight was stowed below on the main deck and in the holds. Nearly as large as the side-wheel palace steamers, *Peerless* carried twin stacks just aft of amidships over her 400-hp engine. A pair of arched hog trusses stiffened the hull, keeping the bow and stern from drooping.

Smaller and more efficient steam engines came to pass during the propeller era. Two-cylinder compound engines, in which steam was expanded twice, made their debut on the Lakes in 1869. Triple-expansion engines appeared in 1887, followed by quadruple-expansion engines in 1894. Each succeeding generation provided incremental improvements in speed, efficiency, and power.

The discovery in 1972 of *Indiana*, which sank in Lake Superior in 1858, has led to a greater understanding of early propeller designs. Built in 1848 by Joseph M. Keating at Vermillion, Ohio, she was 144'½" LOD, with a 23' beam and 10'10" depth. On June 6, 1858, she cleared Lighthouse Point at Marquette, Michigan, and set a northeasterly course for Whitefish Bay. Aboard were a crew of seventeen, three passengers, and 280 tons of iron ore stowed in piles on the main deck. Off Point Crisp Lighthouse, just west of Whitefish Point, she foundered and sank, but without loss of life.

Over a century later, marine archaeologists dived on the wreck, which they found sitting upright on the lake bed, and recorded her characteristics: straight stem, rounded stern, two decks (one large and unobstructed for freight), cargo hold, nearly vertical sides amidships, and minimal sheer. Typical of the early propellers, *Indiana* was powered by an aft-mounted, single-cylinder engine. Investigating the boat up close in Lake Superior's frigid waters led to an understanding of the propeller era that could not have been achieved in any other way.

The large propeller *Westmoreland*—200'2¾" LOA, with a 28'2¾" beam and a 12'¾" depth—was launched in 1853 in the Lafrinier & Stevenson shipyard at Cleveland. In early December 1854,

Early in her career (1872), *Peerless* was a winsome propeller steamer running between Chicago, Illinois, and Duluth, Minnesota, for the Leopold and Austrian Lake Superior Line and, later on, between Chicago and Milwaukee, Wisconsin, for the Chicago Transportation Company. Her main saloon (right) stretched 166', with passenger cabins opening to the saloon. In 1910, she burned and was abandoned. COURTESY OF THUNDER BAY NATIONAL MARINE SANCTUARY, C. PATRICK LABADIE COLLECTION

she loaded cargo and passengers in Chicago, bound up Lake Michigan for Mackinac Island and Buffalo. On Wednesday, December 6, the *Westmoreland* drove into a heavy snowstorm and steep seas and began leaking off the Michigan shore.

By the following afternoon, matters became dire with the steamer taking on water in Platte Bay south of the Manitou Islands. Captain Thomas Clark ordered passengers and crew into three lifeboats and two small yawls. As the vessel went under, a large lifeboat overturned with fifteen passengers and crew who perished in the frigid waters. Two others also lost their lives. The Chicago *Journal* lamented: "With the present Railroad facilities, it is unnecessary to hazard life and property on the lakes at this season of the year."

The loss of the *Westmoreland* might have remained a footnote in Great Lakes history had it not been for rumors during the next 150 years that the ship had carried a strongbox containing $100,000 in $20 double-eagle gold pieces and 350 barrels of whiskey. The *Westmoreland* was discovered in 2010 by Grand Rapids, Michigan, diver and historian Ross Richardson, but he found no gold or whiskey.

"MOSQUITO" STEAMERS

A vintage postcard from the early 1900s depicts the propeller steamer *Hum* underway on a calm summer's day on Michigan's Pine Lake (later called Lake Charlevoix), with a full complement of passengers. The image is an iconic snapshot of maritime life common across the Great Lakes in the nineteenth and early twentieth centuries. The steamer was then owned by Captain George Jepson, who had transitioned from schooners in the late 1880s.

The propeller-driven *Hum* steamed between East Jordan and Charlevoix, Michigan, on Pine Lake, making twice-daily trips with passengers and freight between 1900 and 1917.
AUTHOR'S COLLECTION

Small steamers like *Hum*, primarily propellers under 120' in length, carried passengers and freight throughout the Great Lakes region. These short-haul waterborne buses and trucks of their time were known collectively as the "mosquito fleet," though the boats varied greatly in size and design.

By the 1860s, long-distance steamer routes from Buffalo to Chicago and Milwaukee gave way to year-round travel by railroad, which was faster and not as dependent on weather conditions to maintain regular timetables. But unpretentious mosquito craft remained popular alternatives to uncomfortable horse-drawn vehicles over rough roads at small ports not yet linked by rail.

Lake Charlevoix, which runs inland from the northeast shore of Upper Lake Michigan, had a fleet of small propeller vessels representative of the type throughout the Great Lakes. Several steam packets ran on the lake from the late 1860s into the twentieth century.

By 1890, Captain Jepson was the owner and master of small, short-haul steamers running between East Jordan and Charlevoix on Lake Charlevoix. In 1899, he purchased the small steamer *Walter Crysler*—55' LOA, with an 11' beam and 5' depth—which carried passengers and freight between the two communities. Captain Jepson had recently moved his young family from Manistee, including my grandfather, George Henderson Jepson, to the area, initially to Boyne City and then Charlevoix. By mid-decade, he had settled his family and business in East Jordan on the South Arm of Lake Charlevoix. The East Jordan and Charlevoix Line made regular daily roundtrip runs between East Jordan and Charlevoix, carrying passengers and freight. In addition, the steamers ran special excursions on weekends and holidays to events in communities on Pine Lake and towns on Lake Michigan like Harbor Springs.

In 1901, Jepson acquired the steamer *Pilgrim*—76' LOA, with a 16' beam and 5' depth—one of the last wooden mosquitoes, running between East Jordan and Charlevoix until just before America entered World War I in 1917. The vessel was originally built as the sail and steam yacht *Truant* for Michigan businessman and congressman John S. Newberry, who once entertained President Ulysses S. Grant aboard. Renamed *Pilgrim* by a new owner in 1893, she was rebuilt as a passenger steamer at Grand Haven, Michigan, in 1900 and sold to Captain Jepson a year later. An 85-hp non-condensing

Captain George Jepson next to the pilothouse aboard the mosquito steamer *Pilgrim*, circa 1900, before the vessel was renamed *Hum*. AUTHOR'S COLLECTION

engine drove the vessel, with a single deck forward, a double deck aft of a pilothouse, and a stack amidships. In 1905, he renamed her *Hum* after a close friend's young daughter, nicknamed "Hum," because she always hummed to her dolls. The steamer's sound, when underway, reminded him of the little girl. Tragically, Captain Jepson died unexpectedly that October and control of the business fell to my great-grandmother, Florence, who was well ahead of the times as an influential businesswoman in northern Michigan.

During the sailing season, my grandfather worked aboard the *Hum* in various positions, from collecting tickets to running the coal-fired steam power plant or steering the boat from the second-deck pilothouse. And soon after turning fifteen, he became the vessel's informal master. To comply with the law, Florence employed a licensed captain until young Captain Jepson reached his majority in 1911 and earned his master's papers.

Running opposite *Hum* on the East Jordan and Charlevoix route was the *Joseph Gordon*—43' LOA, with a 9'2" beam and 4'3" depth—powered by a 120-hp non-condensing engine. The *Gordon*, built in West Bay City, Michigan, in 1881, was abandoned in 1907 after her engine and machinery were removed. Although the *Hum* and *Gordon* were separately owned, they were "more complementary than competitive boats," according to Great Lakes maritime historian Dr. William Lafferty.

Mosquito steamers were generally built for coastal and inland waters rather than the open Great Lakes. Shipbuilders in port towns and villages along the Lakes built mosquitoes along with the larger vessels used for cross-lake service until the demand for wooden craft diminished in favor of steel in the waning years of the nineteenth century.

In 1910, the Jepsons rebuilt *Hum* to carry passengers and freight on Lake Michigan to destinations like Beaver Island. Five years later, the Jepson family sold the steamer to a Chicago party, where she sailed as an excursion vessel.

Although propellers dominated the mosquito fleets, a few small paddle steamers operated within the fleet. For example, the *May Graham*—95'7" LOD, with a 16' beam and 3'6" depth—was built in 1879 at St. Joseph, Michigan, along the southwestern shore of Lake Michigan. This two-deck side-wheeler was once a fixture on the St. Joseph River, steaming between Berrien Springs and Benton Harbor. Other paddle-wheel mosquitoes operated on Green Bay in Wisconsin and Lake Macatawa, which flows into Lake Michigan at Holland, Michigan.

Young George Henderson Jepson, circa 1905, about the time he became the Hum's unofficial master following his father's death. AUTHOR'S COLLECTION

As the Buffalo-to-Chicago and -Milwaukee routes gave way to rail travel in the decades following the Civil War, cross-lake excursion traffic was also on the rise, particularly on Lake Michigan. Maritime communities were strung around the lake like so many pearls on a necklace. Steamer routes connected Chicago with western Michigan ports like St. Joseph, South Haven, Muskegon, and Manistee, while Milwaukee and Manitowoc were Wisconsin destinations. Roundtrip excursions aboard the luxurious propeller steamers *Meteor* and *Pewabic* embarked from Cleveland and Detroit, carrying passengers up the lakes through the St. Mary's River to Lake Superior. These trips offered scenic views of the Thousand Isles and Pictured Rocks en route to Marquette, the first iron ore port on the Great Lakes.

Wooden side-wheelers and propellers, including the "mosquito fleet" vessels (see sidebar on page 53), were built in many of these ports. The propeller *H.W. Williams*—140' LOD, with a 28' beam and 10'4" depth—rose from the stocks in John B. Martel's

The propeller steamers *Meteor* and *Pewabic* boasted new and luxurious upper-deck cabins in this broadside, promoting cruises to Lake Superior as the American Civil War ended. COURTESY OF THUNDER BAY NATIONAL MARINE SANCTUARY, C. PATRICK LABADIE COLLECTION

The propeller *City of Kalamazoo* slid down the ways into the Black River in 1893 at South Haven, Michigan, and carried revelers from Michigan to the Chicago World's Fair (World's Columbian Exposition). COURTESY OF THUNDER BAY NATIONAL MARINE SANCTUARY, C. PATRICK LABADIE COLLECTION

South Haven, Michigan, shipyard in 1888. She initially ran between South Haven and Chicago. The Martel-built propeller *City of Kalamazoo*—161'8" LOD, with a 31'10" beam and 12'6" depth—splashed into the Black River in 1893, in time to carry crowds of revelers to the Chicago World's Fair (World's Columbian Exposition). These vessels, representative of similar craft throughout the Lakes, continued steaming into the 1920s, well after the wooden ship–building yards were replaced by steel ship-building concerns.

Wooden steamers trailing clouds of black smoke operated on the Great Lakes for over a century. They vanished long ago, but their legacy lives on in the villages and towns that swelled with new generations of enterprising Americans and immigrants delivered to the shores of the Great Lakes during the nineteenth century.

D. F. Rose, a 140' LOD "rabbit"-configured steam barge with two consorts in tow, was built by George Koening in 1868 at Marine City, Michigan, and served until 1910.

COURTESY OF THUNDER BAY NATIONAL MARINE SANCTUARY, C. PATRICK LABADIE COLLECTION

CHAPTER 3

Steam Barges
BUILDING A YOUNG NATION

Under a flawless sky, black smudge poured from the steam barge *Trader*'s stack. Downbound on Lake Huron in midsummer 1865, she had a hawser out with three additional barges in tow, all of them schooner-rigged but with furled sails, looking much like ducklings behind their mother. Plowing through a mild chop, this small propeller-driven steamer—115' LOD, with a 22'6" beam and 8'7" draft—and her consorts were loaded in hold and on deck with lumber from Michigan's Saginaw Valley, destined for the market in Buffalo, New York.

The last battlefields of the Civil War had fallen silent only a few months earlier, and America's hunger for lumber—some called it "green gold"— was voracious (see sidebar, page 66). Michigan, at the time, had emerged as the principal lumber-producing state in the Union, since forests farther east had already been depleted. The forests of the West Coast were, for the time being, still too far away to exploit effectively. To meet the nation's insatiable demands for raw logs and finished products (planks, laths, shingles, cedar posts, telegraph poles, and railroad ties), Michigan's timber companies had to find a way to move large quantities of wood products to trading and trans-shipment centers throughout the Great Lakes.

Trader opened a new era in shipping. An innovative type of steam barge, she was designed not only to carry a bulk cargo of her own—up to 250,000 board feet of lumber—but also to tow several barge-like sailing schooners which were

"Lumber shovers" unload the *Langell Boys*, 151' LOD, and a second unidentified steam barge in Bay City, Michigan, in 1905.
COURTESY OF THUNDER BAY NATIONAL MARINE SANCTUARY

themselves loaded with immense cargoes. The idea was to keep costs low by shipping in bulk, which increasingly was becoming the principal trade for Great Lakes steamers. As late as 1878, *Trader* was purchased by the Pentwater (Michigan) Lumber Company to run twice weekly on Lake Michigan from Pentwater to Chicago to Milwaukee. Even then, fully eighteen years into her working life, the *Pentwater News* described her as a "neat, trim staunch looking boat . . . finely built" with "excellent sea-going qualities" enabling "her to make good time." *Trader* had a single, open cargo deck with small cabins aft, topped by a pilothouse. The steam engine was also mounted aft over the keel, with the smokestack rising above and behind the pilothouse. Close to the bow, a tall mast carried a gaff-rigged sail and a jib, providing stability in a blow or auxiliary power to take advantage of a favorable wind. This type of steam barge became known as a "rabbit." A mark of her success was that the same type continued to be built through the 1870s, supplanted only by larger steam barges in the succeeding decades.

THE FIRST STEAM BARGES

In an earlier generation, before the Civil War, efforts to move bulk cargoes in steam barges had been tried, but with limited success. Until the 1840s, schooners had been the primary workhorses for carrying bulk commodities such as lumber. Before *Trader* slid down the ways at Marine City, Michigan, in early 1865, the steamers of the time, powered by side-wheels or propellers, were best suited to the lucrative trade of transporting passengers and package freight, though on occasion they also carried bulk cargo in small quantities.

Watercraft designs on the Great Lakes evolved with each succeeding generation of shipbuilders to meet the inland sea's geographical and environmental challenges: shallow and confined waters, few natural harbors, narrow shipping canals, and often treacherous seas.

By the end of the 1840s, shipwrights had begun to build experimental propeller-driven steamers specifically for the lumber trade, though they remained a rarity on the Lakes before the end of the Civil War. These steam barges were built within specific dimensions, not more than 142'5" LOA nor more than 26'3" in the beam, so they could transit the Welland Canal linking Lake Ontario and Lake Erie.

Petrel, which was considered the first of the steam barges, was launched in 1848 at Joseph Arnold's shipyard at Port Huron, Michigan. At 118' LOD, with a 23'8" beam and 9' draft, she was a precursor to what later were known as "rabbit-configured" steam barges like *Trader*. Despite their perceived strengths, *Petrel* and vessels like her proved unprofitable for moving lumber. *Petrel* was soon put to work hauling other bulk cargoes until she foundered on Lake Erie in 1850, ending her short life.

Efforts to make steamers pay in the bulk cargo trade continued, however. On October 6, 1853, the *Buffalo Morning Express* reported sighting "a rather odd-looking propeller christened *Pacific* . . . built [expressly] for the lumber trade" on the waterfront. She was a small rabbit—93'7" LOD, with an 18' beam and 7'3" draft—built in Racine, Wisconsin. But a year later, she was converted to sail, using a two-masted schooner rig.

During this same period, American and Canadian shipwrights experimented with small steamers configured like rabbits but with side-wheels. These so-called pollywogs, with paddle boxes located on either side of the aft cabins and pilothouse, navigated shallow tributaries flowing into the Great Lakes, carrying lumber and other bulk freight. The *George Moffat*, a 135' LOA with a 24' beam and an 11' draft, was built at Chatham, Ontario, in 1853, and operated on Lake Erie, Lake Ontario, and the St. Lawrence River until 1864. Pollywogs proved not entirely suited for open waters, limiting their value compared to propeller-driven steam barges.

TWISTS OF FATE

As the American economy spun into the economic abyss of the Panic of 1857, merchant ship owners fought to survive. Many went bankrupt. Especially hard-hit were the passenger and package-freight businesses. The hard times left schooners and steamers idle, and many of them slowly rotted at their berths. In this failure, enterprising shipping company owners realized that these vessels could be purchased cheap, cut down by removing their superstructures, and refitted as tow barges, with considerable capacities for carrying lumber. Larger cargoes, they reckoned, would result in lower shipping costs.

In 1862, John S. Noyes of Buffalo, New York, purchased the once-elegant passenger steamers *Sultana* and *Empire* and converted them into tow barges, giving them rudimentary sloop rigs. They were very large: *Sultana* was 217'4" LOD, with a beam of 30'7" and a 12'8" draft. *Empire* was even larger, 253'6" LOD, with a beam of 32'8" and a 14'2" draft. They had cargo capacities five times that of the period's propeller steamers. Noyes used the tugboat *Reindeer* (101'6" LOD, with a 22'9" beam and 10' draft) to tow strings of such barges from the Saginaw River in Michigan to Buffalo, bearing enormous loads of lumber.

Economic shifts continued during the war. One fundamental change was the rapid westward expansion of railroads, which drew even more of the lucrative passenger and package-freight trade

Albert Soper, 143'6" LOD, slid down the ways in 1881 at Duncan Robertson's yard at Grand Haven, Michigan. She was a regular in the Lake Michigan lumber trade until 1916, when she was sold into the West Indies trade. Four years later she sank in the Caribbean Sea. COURTESY OF THUNDER BAY NATIONAL MARINE SANCTUARY

away from the Great Lakes schooners and steamers. This came as a blow to ship owners, who were increasingly left with the less-lucrative bulk cargo trade. But few existing vessels were suited to carry such commodities in quantities large enough to make a profit, especially given the limitations of the canal system.

On March 31, 1864, the *Detroit Free Press* proclaimed: "The class of vessels most earnestly sought are those best adapted for the lumber trade . . . a dozen more would meet with ready sale." So, shipwrights along the Detroit and St. Clair Rivers rolled up their sleeves and went to work, and more steam barges gradually took shape on the stocks.

N. Mills, 164'5", was an early pilothouse-forward steam barge. Built by Philander Lester at Vicksburg (now Marysville), Michigan, in 1870, she is shown in 1901 with fully laden schooner barges in tow. She sank in the St. Clair River in 1906. COURTESY OF THUNDER BAY NATIONAL MARINE SANCTUARY

Very quickly after the Civil War ended, the country's demand for building materials—particularly softwoods from timber-rich Michigan—went from robust to nearly insatiable. Moreover, Reconstruction was underway in the South. Cities, villages, and small towns across the land were growing, fueled by immigration and expansion westward to the prairies and beyond. Sawmills buzzed incessantly on the banks of rivers flowing to the Lakes, filling the air with the resinous scent of sawdust. Schooners, steamers, and steam barges by the hundreds swarmed the Saginaw River in Michigan, waiting to load lumber for markets and trans-shipment centers in Ohio, New York, and Chicago.

Noyes's "consort system" quickly took hold once the disruptions caused by the Civil War had passed. During the 1860s, dozens of obsolete passenger steamers were refitted as barges, carrying one or two masts. Likewise, old, obsolete schooners, with much-reduced rigs, were pressed back into service for the same purpose. Noyes's idea initiated a transportation system that could deliver looming quantities of lumber to the marketplace at low cost.

At first, tugboats towed the sailing barges, but soon shipyards began constructing self-propelled steam barges specifically for the lumber trade. After *Trader*'s launching in 1865, the fleet of steam barges grew steadily. During the next five years, forty-five new rabbits were built, and twenty propeller steamers were refitted as steam barges. These "lumber hooker" steam barges, whose hulls resembled those of the schooners they were designed to tow, carried their own cargoes of lumber and replaced the tugs as towboats. Fully loaded themselves and pulling a string of fully loaded consorts, they could achieve 6 to 8 mph. Moreover, these barges required only small crews, keeping wages, and therefore costs, low. Tows generally consisted of three or four barges, but more powerful steam barges could pull more. For example, *Antelope*—186' LOD, with a 31' beam and an 11' draft—regularly hauled eight fully loaded barges, a string that stretched nearly a mile. Clearly, the steam barge's time had come, and the new system sparked a revolution in Great Lakes shipping.

Although running steam barges towing a string of unpowered barges was inexpensive, loading them was labor-intensive, costly, and inefficient. "Lumber shoving" involved passing lumber from a dockside woodpile to the ship. Lumber shovers, wearing canvas aprons and harvest mitts as protection against splinters, started work in the early morning darkness. Men ashore passed twelve-foot-long boards to men on deck, who in turn passed them through a hatch to more men down in the hold. Once the hold was filled, lumber was stacked five to ten feet high on deck. The grueling workday, which often included loading more than one ship, ended at sundown. "In order to determine whether a ship was fully loaded, a crewman would walk from side to side across the top of the stacked lumber, and if the ship listed, loading was complete," said maritime historian Patrick Labadie (see sidebar on page 68), recalling a conversation he had with a former steam barge crewman.

THE GREAT LAKES LUMBER BOOM ERA

The Great Lakes lumber boom exploded in the 1860s, by which time forests in the previous leading lumber-producing states—New York, Maine, Pennsylvania, Ohio, and South Carolina—were nearly depleted. The lumber trade converged on Michigan, which then had abundant stands of virgin timber that could satisfy America's demand for construction materials. The lumber industry in Michigan was built primarily on softwoods such as white pine, Norway pine, and jack pine, as well as the less-valued spruce, white cedar, tamarack, and hemlock. Pine, particularly white pine, was the most highly prized species. The rush started in the Saginaw Valley. Over the next thirty years, virtually the entire Lower Peninsula of Michigan above the 43rd Parallel was logged off.

Blessed with a network of rivers running from deep inland, loggers had natural swift-water routes by which logs could be floated downstream to sawmills. During winter, felled logs, stacked in tall pyramids on sleds, were pulled to the riverbanks over snow and ice by teams of oxen or horses. In the spring, the logs were rolled into the waterways and carried downstream to the mills. On some rivers, logs cut long distances from sawmills were often bundled into great rafts or "booms," and towed downriver by small steamers. Freshly milled boards—sometimes referred to as "deals"—were loaded aboard steam barges, tow barges, and schooners for shipment to New York, Ohio, and Illinois market centers. At the time, Chicago, the gateway to the West, was the greatest lumber market in the world. During the 1860s, deliveries to the Windy City from Michigan and Wisconsin sawmills quadrupled. The Port of Chicago teemed with vessels bringing lumber for shipment by rail to towns and villages all over Illinois and Iowa, where wood resources were scarce.

On October 8, 1871, fire swept across Chicago, and unrelated fires simultaneously raged through northeastern Wisconsin and Lower Michigan, destroying timber across millions of acres. The demand for lumber to rebuild Chicago was staggering. Practically all the sawmills in Michigan responded to the strong market, despite losing so much forestland in the state's own devastating fires. In Singapore, a small village on the Kalamazoo River near Saugatuck and Douglas, Michigan, the local sawmill cut down every tree in the vicinity, including all those on the coastal dunes bordering Lake Michigan. This proved disastrous: Four years later, the town disappeared under shifting sands, where it still lies today, a footnote in history. The financial Panic of 1873, which ignited in the autumn, barely affected the lumber industry. Although small businesses were frequently driven from the trade, bigger ones thrived. Despite hard times, America's westward expansion continued. By the 1880s, sawmills from Michigan's Upper Peninsula, Wisconsin, and Minnesota were shipping even more lumber to the markets.

In 1888, Michigan's lumber industry reached its peak, producing 4.29 billion board feet. The annual output declined afterward, although the state still led the nation until the late 1890s. Then Michigan fell to second place behind Wisconsin, which briefly became the top lumber-producing state before the honor was passed to states in the Pacific Northwest.

Thousands of loads of white pine logs, like these loaded pyramid fashion on a horse-drawn sled in 1890, were taken to rivers to be floated to sawmills which then shipped lumber via steam barges to market. COURTESY OF THUNDER BAY NATIONAL MARINE SANCTUARY

PAT LABADIE AND SHIPWRECK RESEARCH

As a young man in the late 1950s, C. Patrick Labadie contemplated a career as a naval architect until esteemed maritime historian Howard Chapelle suggested that a career in a maritime museum would better serve his interests than "designing plastic boats." Labadie took his advice.

Investigating Great Lakes shipwrecks up close and researching a bygone era became his passion in the years ahead. An experienced Great Lakes diver, Labadie spent considerable time exploring and preserving shipwrecks on Lake Huron as a historian at the Thunder Bay National Marine Sanctuary in Alpena, Michigan. Earlier in his career, he served as director of the Duluth (Minnesota) Lake Superior Marine Museum, now called the Duluth Maritime Visitor's Center. Labadie's grandfather, who worked in wooden shipyards, inspired his interest, which grew while collaborating with University of Detroit historian Father Edward Dowling.

Over half a century later, the soft-spoken historian and underwater archaeologist is an authority on ships of the Inland Seas, especially wooden vessels of the mid-nineteenth century. A rewarding aspect of his work has been diving on shipwrecks, including thirteen steam barges, to examine firsthand the methods and materials used by shipwrights. "Uncovering things that were not recorded in a ship's plans," Labadie explained, "provides insights into construction techniques that might not be revealed anywhere else. Variation was great from builder to builder. There was an enormous variety among individual vessels." Combining this information with historical documents and period photos has allowed him to create detailed descriptions of ships from another time. Among these vessels were:

For more than half a century, Pat Labadie, former historian at the Thunder Bay National Marine Sanctuary in Alpena, Michigan, on Lake Huron, studied nineteenth- and twentieth-century Great Lakes ships. His data and images are archived in Alpena County's George N. Fletcher Library.

- *ADVENTURE*, a rabbit-configured steam barge, 120'6" LOD, with a 24' beam and an 8'3" draft, built as a schooner in 1875 and fitted out as a "lumber hooker" in 1897. Fire destroyed her on October 6, 1903, at Kelleys Island, Ohio. Labadie gathered enough information to create drawings illustrating her hull structure when diving on the ship. Not surprisingly, it was built very much like a schooner.

- *B. W. BLANCHARD*, a Western Transportation Company package freighter converted to a steam barge after thirty years of service. Exploring this ship allowed Labadie to study the conversion, including the vessel's cumbersome hogging arches. At 212'4" LOD, with a 32'5" beam and 12'2" draft, this was one of the largest vessels to sail in the lumber trade.

Unfortunately, she burned and sank on September 6, 1914.

Great Lakes maritime historians, fortunately, have easy access to shipwrecks today, where laws ban the recovery of artifacts. In the cold depths of the freshwater seas—especially in Lake Superior—hulls are well preserved, opening windows into the past. Divers are often able to swim inside hulls. Describing typical shipwrecks, Labadie explained that "their sides frequently collapse outward, revealing internal structural details that are normally hidden from view." His first dives permitted only twenty to thirty minutes of working time, but technology has advanced since then. Today, daylong probes with ROVs—remote-operated vehicles—are routine. And operators working from the surface can capture details on camera and use lasers to take measurements.

Labadie has spent decades combing through historical records and ships' plans, gathering photos, and reading personal accounts by shipwrights and sailors. His work has culminated in the Thunder Bay Research Collection, with sixty thousand period photographs, fifteen thousand ship histories, contemporary anecdotes, newspaper articles, and shipwreck documentation. All are available online at www.greatlakesships.org.

THE BOOM YEARS

The pace of ship construction only accelerated in the final decades of the nineteenth century. Estimates show that nearly eight hundred steam barges, ranging in size from 80' to 200' LOD, were launched between 1870 and 1910. Although initially built for the lumber business, steam barges also came to carry other bulk cargoes such as iron, coal, sand, and grain. The consort period, however, was dangerous on the Great Lakes, particularly late in the season with autumnal storms, when the sweetwater seas could turn perilous without warning. Heavily laden barges were top-heavy and unwieldy craft. If a barge was separated from its steam barge or another consort, it had little chance of riding out a storm. Mishaps often resulted in tragedy.

On September 28, 1895, a storm from the northwest swept the length of Lake Superior. At the eastern end of the lake, the steam barge *P.H. Birckhead*—156'9" LOD, with a 27'10" beam and a 13'5" depth—and three consorts were caught off Whitefish Point. Heavily loaded with milled lumber bound for the market on the lower lakes, the

The *Charles W. Bradley* was built in West Bay City, Michigan, in 1890 and steamed the Great Lakes in the lumber trade until 1931, when she was struck by her consort, *Grampian*, caught fire, and burned to the waterline. Shown with a schooner barge in tow, she also carried a schooner rig for stability in a blow or auxiliary power.

COURTESY OF THUNDER BAY NATIONAL MARINE SANCTUARY

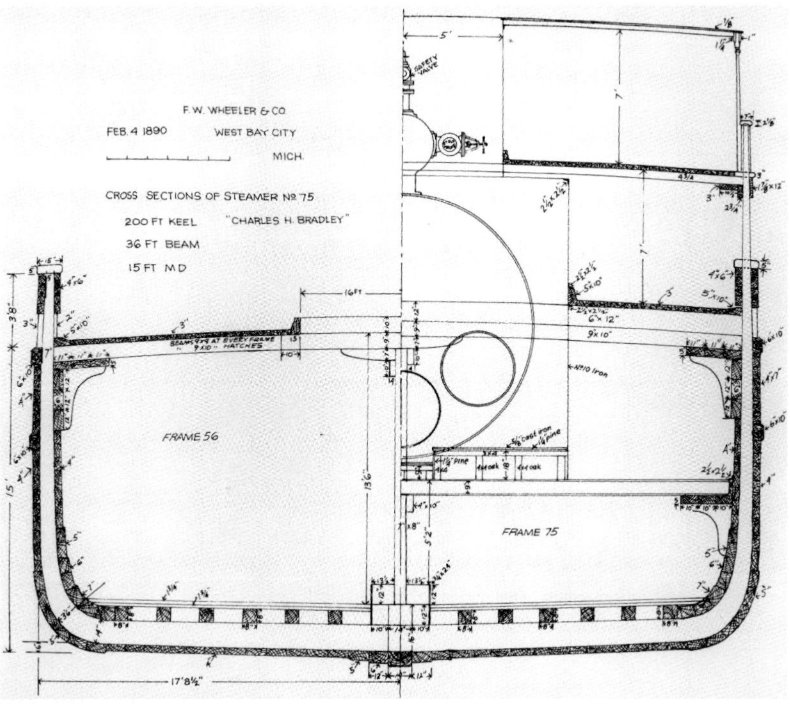

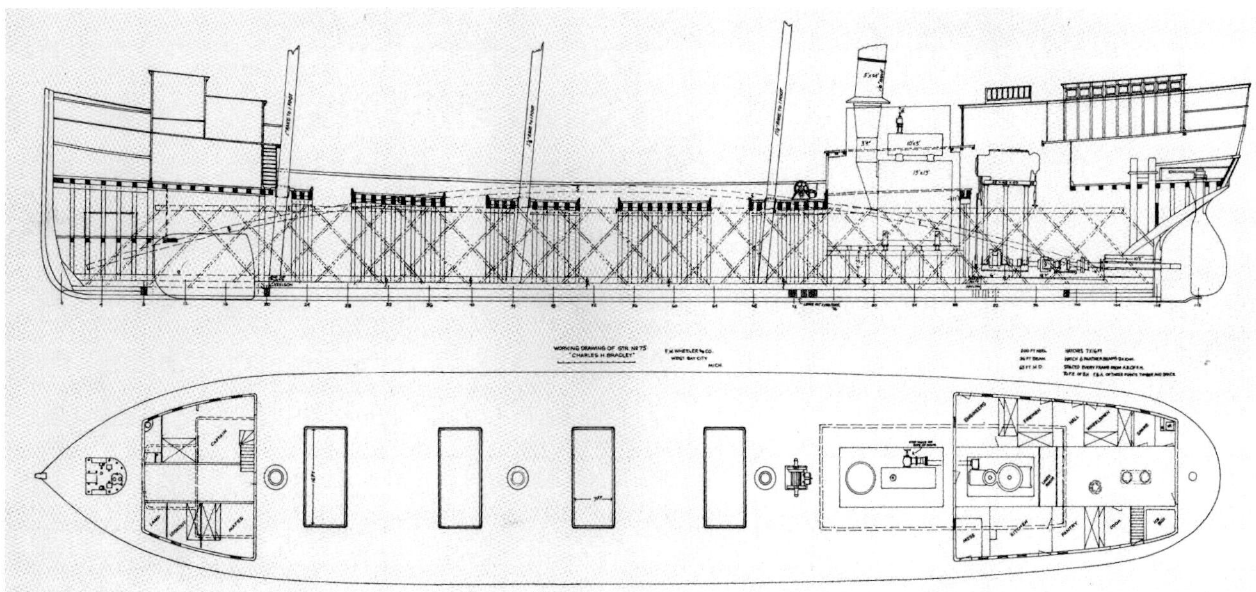

The *Charles W. Bradley*, 201' LOD, was one of the largest steam barges operating on the Great Lakes. A close look at her profile (bottom) reveals a centerboard forward, diagonal strapping along her sides, and an internal arch to increase the ship's longitudinal strength. A cross section (top) shows her single deck and substantial keelson assembly.

four vessels were no match for the tempest. The towline connecting the ship to the first barge parted, setting the entire string loose. The crews cut their towlines as the barges foundered in heavy seas. One barge escaped under shortened sail down Whitefish Bay toward Sault Ste. Marie. A second came to her anchor just offshore. *Birckhead* was able to pass a hawser to the third, then struck a westerly course for Grand Island, some eighty miles away. But with high seas running, the towline parted again off Pictured Rocks near Munising. The wind drove the barge ashore onto a rocky reef while the steam barge found shelter behind Grand Island. Although one consort was lost—along with the life of one seaman—the other two barges and the steam barge survived. This episode was typical of the risks encountered on the Great Lakes. By the 1890s, shipping interests and the Life-Saving Services in the United States and Canada realized that tow barges were often undermanned with unskilled crews. Long strings of barges were hazards to navigation, particularly in storms when vessels foundered, often with loss of life. Ship owners were not

A crewman aboard the *Edwin S. Tice*, 159'11" LOD, decked out in oilskins, stands atop a deck load of raw logs. Launched in 1887 at the H. B. & G. B. Burger shipyard in Manitowoc, Wisconsin, she operated in the lumber business on Lakes Michigan and Superior until 1933. COURTESY OF THUNDER BAY NATIONAL MARINE SANCTUARY

deterred by these matters, however, because financial losses were easily absorbed.

Steam barges voyaging without tows could also be in jeopardy on the Great Lakes. In 1880, *Trader* was lost on Lake Michigan during a run between Chicago and Muskegon, Michigan. The schooner *City of Grand Haven* reported passing through her wreckage off Grand Haven, Michigan. A notice appearing in the October 19, 1880, *Kingston Whig-Standard* said: "The steam barge *Trader* . . . has gone to pieces on the east shore . . . Capt. Brown and a crew of ten probably perished."

STEAM BARGE CONSTRUCTION

At first glance, steam barges physically resembled the much larger wooden bulk freighters that entered Great Lakes service in the early 1870s, with the launch of the *R. J. Hackett* (see Chapter 4, "Bulk Freighters: America's Long Ships"). The two vessel types often created confusion in maritime literature of the period, as it was common for the term "steam barge" to be used to describe both of

them until, in the 1880s, the phrase "bulk carrier" came into common use.

Physical appearance aside, steam barge hulls, built with white oak, were significantly different from those of the wooden bulk freighters. Archaeological teams examining original ship plans and diving on submerged steam barge wrecks in the Great Lakes (see sidebar, page 68, "Pat Labadie and Shipwreck Research") have documented many similarities in design and construction between schooners and steam barges. Vessels of both types were characterized by heavy centerline keelson assemblies, double-sawn frames, and longitudinal ceiling planking. Shoal-draft schooners were also equipped with centerboards, which were also found on many steam barges. In order to support the weight of engines and boilers, steam barges were built with up to two additional sister keelsons on either side of the centerline, much like bulk freighters. In addition, external hogging arches or trusses were standard features on the early steam barges and freighters, minimizing the stress on hulls created by machinery or heavy cargoes. By the 1880s, hulls were reinforced with iron strapping mortised into frames in a diagonal, crisscrossed pattern.

Iconic Great Lakes freighter pilothouses mounted on the foredeck appeared in the early 1870s, but became standard on steam barges by the 1880s, providing much-improved visibility for the master and helmsman. Crew quarters and a galley remained aft, with a well deck extending between bow and stern. While earlier steam barges carried single masts near the bow, the newer and larger models were fitted with two or three masts that could be rigged with working sails. Despite general characteristics common to all steam barges, whether rabbits or the later types with their pilothouses forward, steam barge construction varied according to the whims of their builders.

THE 1880s FORWARD

The lumber boom in Michigan's Lower Peninsula peaked around 1880. By then, lumber was flowing down rivers to ports from Saginaw on the eastern side of the mitten-shaped state around the peninsula to Muskegon on the western side. Along the shore, shipbuilders produced steam barges to meet regional lumber shipping demands. Muskegon, located at the mouth of the two-hundred-mile-long Muskegon River, was called "the Lumber Queen of the World." A keen observer during this period was newspaper editor and historian James L. Smith, who wrote, "The steam barges began to capture the lumber-carrying trade in a limited way in the later years of the '70s. I recall regular visits of two rather small steam lumber carriers, [one of which was] the *George Dunbar*. They were gradually followed by quite a fleet of steam barges. Adverse winds seldom interfered seriously with the round trips to lumber distribution centers by the steam barges."

Captain H. C. Inches, who was born in 1882 and spent much of his boyhood in shipyards along the St. Clair River, sailed with his father aboard wooden ships and was later a master of Great Lakes bulk freighters. "Our ships on the lakes were made of the finest white oak," he wrote. "Even at that, our good oak ships were at their best only for 15 years." Ships that weren't lost in storms or

White Swan, 81' LOD, a small Washington Island lumber hooker launched in 1923 by Burger Boat Company in Manitowoc, Wisconsin, was a compact rabbit. She was among the last of the steam barge breed, operating off Wisconsin until 1956 when she foundered and was lost in Lake Michigan.
COURTESY OF THUNDER BAY NATIONAL MARINE SANCTUARY

collisions ultimately succumbed to decay. As a result, shipbuilders, often located up rivers and away from the lakes, were pressed to maintain the steam barge fleet.

As the turn of the twentieth century approached, the Great Lakes lumber trade, which had reached Michigan's Upper Peninsula and northern Wisconsin, was in decline. So too were steam barges, though a few lasted a bit longer. The *M. H. Stuart*—104'6" LOD, with a 25'6" beam and an 8'8" draft—was constructed in the Walter & O'Boyle shipyard at Sturgeon Bay, Wisconsin, and was launched in 1921. *White Swan*—81' LOD, with a 23' beam and a 7'6" draft—was launched in 1922 by Burger Boat Company in Manitowoc, Wisconsin. The *M. H. Stuart* sank in Lake Huron in 1937 and *White Swan* foundered off Île aux Galets in Lake Michigan in 1956.

Small Washington Island lumber hookers (less than 65' LOD) were among the last of the breed, working off Wisconsin on Lake Michigan into the 1930s. Great Lakes maritime historian Henry Barkhausen (see Chapter 8, "Henry Barkhausen: A Great Lakes Mariner Remembers") recalled that they "were small enough so they could operate with only two men. I remember the *Diana* and the *Wisconsin*, and there was, I think, another operating that late."

The legacy of these splendid vessels endures. They are the ancestors of the magnificent bulk freighters that still sail the Great Lakes a century and a half after *Petrel* first tasted fresh water in 1848.

The *William B. Morley* slides down the ways (a side launching) into the St. Clair River at Marine City, Michigan, in 1889. She was one of a breed of vessels that sailed the Great Lakes carrying iron ore, coal, and grain. COURTESY OF THUNDER BAY NATIONAL MARINE SANCTUARY

CHAPTER 4

Bulk Freighters

AMERICA'S LONG SHIPS

Old Glory waved gently under an autumn sky as the wooden propeller steamer *R. J. Hackett* splashed into the Cuyahoga River at Peck & Masters shipyard in Cleveland, Ohio, on November 16, 1869. The long, bluff-bowed ship—208'1" LOA, with a beam of 32'5" and a 12'6" depth of hold—was destined to make Great Lakes maritime history as the standard design for bulk freighters sailing on America's sweetwater seas. Over a year earlier, the *Detroit Free Press* reported in its October 10, 1868, edition: "Mr. E.M. Peck, the well-known shipbuilder of Cleveland, has laid the keel of a new propeller [steamer] of an entirely new design for freight purposes. . . . The peculiarity in design consists chiefly [in] adapting her to all kinds of freight . . . coal, iron ore, grain, etc."

By the following spring, the backbone and frames of the bulk freighter *R. J. Hackett* (the *Hackett*) had risen on the stocks along the southern shore of Lake Erie like the skeleton of an enormous prehistoric creature. Elihu M. Peck (known as Eli) wanted increased cargo space in his ships, and he wanted those ships to be more compatible with the new pocket ore docks at Marquette and Escanaba, Michigan. Pocket docks would allow dockworkers to load ships in a fraction of the time it took to load ships manually.

The *Hackett* would usher in the era of the bulk freighter, more than tripling the cargo capacity of the schooners. In the ensuing months, ships' carpenters shaped planks, joiners built cabins, and caulkers drove home oakum. All the while,

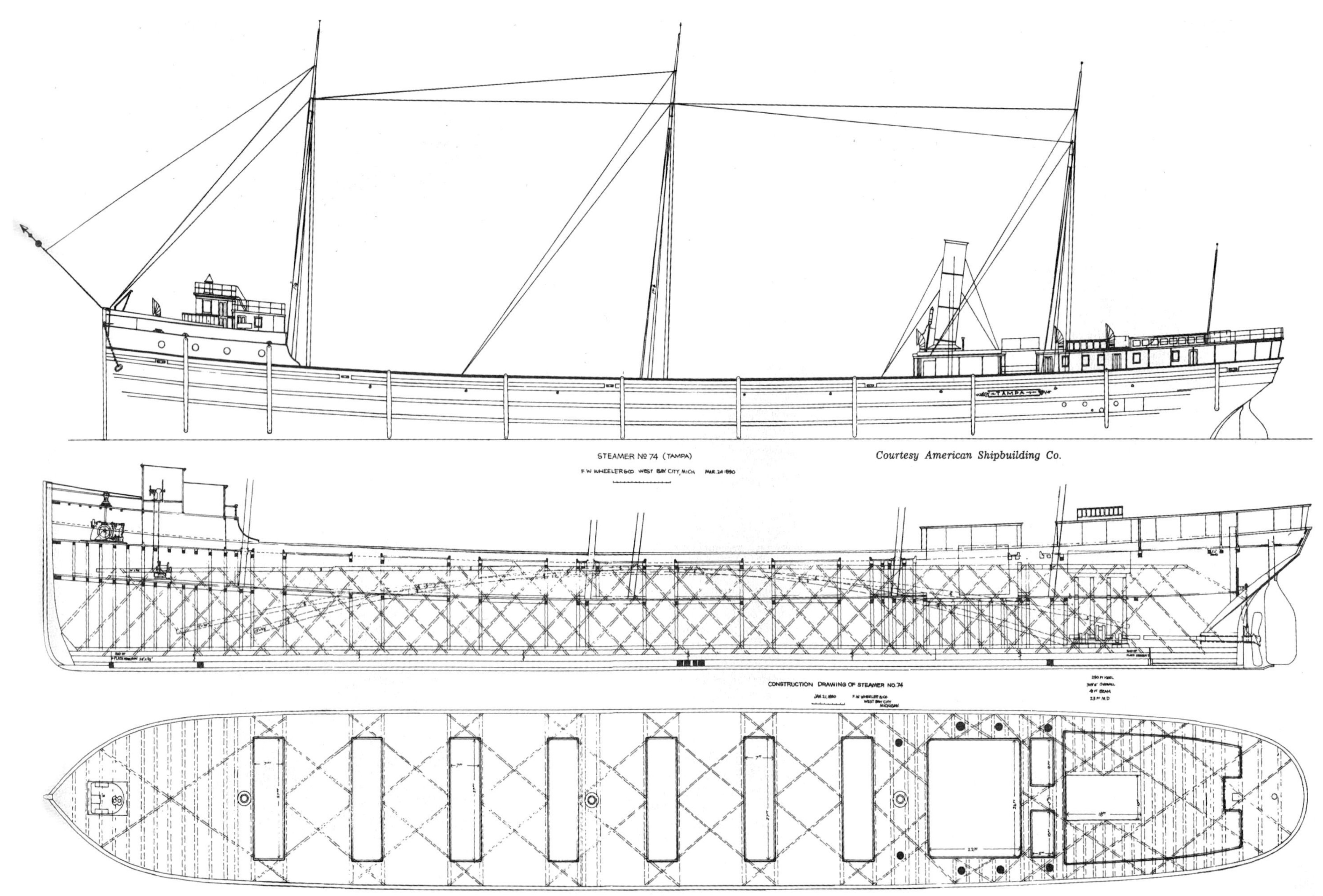

The *R. J. Hackett* shows a pilothouse forward and a cabin aft. The deck featured hatches set on 24' centers to accommodate loading chutes that existed on Michigan's specialized ore docks at the time. COURTESY OF THUNDER BAY NATIONAL MARINE SANCTUARY

waterfront observers— "sidewalk superintendents" of the day—speculated about the vessel's unusual appearance. A fore-and-aft configuration made the *Hackett* unique among steamers of the era. The pilothouse sat near the extreme point of the bow, over crews' quarters, allowing the captain an unobstructed view of narrow, bending channels. An aft cabin containing additional crews' quarters sat over the engine room. The long hull had high sides, a nearly square cross-section, and a round stern. A continuous hold was open from the forecastle to the boiler-room bulkheads. On the open deck, three short gaff-rigged masts were placed to carry sails should the engine fail or the ship require stabilization in a heavy blow. Hatch covers were spaced on 24' centers to line up with the loading chute spacing on the ore docks at Marquette and Escanaba, Michigan.

During this era, Great Lakes shipyards were abuzz with activity. Ship carpenters perched on scaffolding worked long augers into oak timbers, wrestled planks into place, and secured them with massive clamps for fastening. Wood shavings piled up as workmen, deftly wielding broadaxes and adzes, roughed out and faired frames and floor timbers. A medley of aromas and a cacophony of disparate sounds aroused the senses. The scents of steamed white oak filled the air, along with tar and paint, while the steady rhythm of singing crosscut saws and the *thunk, thunk, thunk* of wooden mallets striking "treenails" and caulking irons resonated along the waterfront. Squawking gulls hovered overhead, hoping to capture a scrap from a worker's lunch in the yard.

The men working in shipyards were a hardy breed of professionals who provided their own tools, worked ten-hour shifts, six days a week, and took great pride in the quality and quantity of work they turned out. If shipbuilding slowed or came to a halt, as it did during the economic Panic of 1873, these men would sign on as crew aboard ships they had helped build. During the winters, with traffic on the lakes at a standstill, these same men would trek deep into forests to harvest timber and haul it out for the shipyard.

The *Tampa* (291'7" LOA, 41' beam, 19'10" depth of hold) was among the largest bulk carriers of the wooden freighter era. A close look at her keel reveals several keelsons layered on top of it. Those additional keelsons increased the ship's longitudinal strength. COURTESY OF THUNDER BAY NATIONAL MARINE SANCTUARY

While the *Hackett* was being built at Peck & Masters' yard, a nearby shipyard converted the bark, *William T. Graves*, to a steamship specifically for the Lake Superior iron ore trade. With this refit, the *Grave*'s carrying capacity—like the *Hackett*'s—would surpass one thousand tons, which was significantly greater than the largest schooners of the day. As the *Hackett* settled in the Cuyahoga, Eli Peck satisfied the quest for a ship design to fundamentally change commercial trade in general, and the iron ore trade in particular on the Great Lakes. Even so, skeptics wondered whether this vessel, whose lines were considered ungainly by some, would become "Peck's Folly." These notions of failure scattered to the four winds in the months ahead.

PECK'S VISION

Born in Otsego County, New York, in 1822, Peck was smitten with boats and ships from his earliest years. As a young man, he worked as a ship's carpenter, learning the shipbuilding trade and inspiring him eventually to build ships to his own designs. Peck's vision for the *Hackett* had evolved over more than thirty years of working in shipyards and observing the flow of commerce on the Great Lakes.

By 1847, Peck recognized the need for vessels with greater cargo capacities when he built the schooner *Jenny Lind*—100'2" LOA, with a 20'8" beam and an 8'9" depth of hold—on the banks of the Cuyahoga River in Cleveland. She was given an uncommonly full hull form with a blunt bow, square in cross-section, and a two-hundred-ton capacity, allowing her to carry more cargo than other ships of similar length. *Jenny Lind* sailed

Shipwrights prepare to fit out the hull of a wooden bulk freighter. The stacked keelson is visible as workers clamp massive pieces of bilge ceiling on either side of the long structure. COURTESY OF THUNDER BAY NATIONAL MARINE SANCTUARY

from Cleveland on her maiden voyage in 1848, bound for Buffalo with a load of grain—a major commodity at the time.

Although the need for a big bulk carrier like the *Hackett* was not yet evident, Peck continued to build ever larger ships—primarily barks and propeller steamers—at Cleveland for trade on the lakes. As a result, Peck's yard, though small among Cuyahoga shipyards, became the leader in tonnage constructed between 1849 and 1869, averaging 540 tons per vessel, while his competitors averaged just 168 tons per vessel. In 1855, Peck formed a partnership with Cleveland businessman Irvine U. Masters, creating Peck & Masters and shoring up the shipyard's financial base. While Peck concentrated on designing and building ships, Masters looked after the company's pocketbook. Masters also pursued local politics and was elected mayor of Cleveland in 1863. Sadly, he died the following year, but Peck, in loyalty, retained his name above the company door.

Between 1864 (near the end of the American Civil War) and the launch of the *Hackett*, few ships were built at Peck & Masters, while the carpenters, joiners, spar builders, and riggers in the shipyard repaired and maintained vessels owned by others. Despite having a reputation for being brusque and difficult to approach, Eli Peck showed considerable compassion for his employees. If orders were weak, he often built ships on speculation ensuring the shipyard workers and their families would not suffer. These vessels invariably found buyers.

While the iron ore industry continued to expand (see sidebar on page 91), shipbuilders on the Great Lakes wrestled with the problem of constructing a vessel that was narrow enough to transit the mile-long canal connecting Lake Huron and Lake Superior at Sault Ste. Marie, with holds deep enough and long enough to carry ever more profitable loads of ore from the iron ranges in Michigan and Minnesota. Eli Peck was the first to build such a ship. The *Hackett* was completed on speculation. Potential lenders, who had balked at financing the ship, joined throngs of others in the marine trades in calling her an "ugly duckling." Conventional designs, they argued, were sounder investments.

Fortunately, Peck found a kindred spirit in Captain Robert J. Hackett, a seasoned mariner on the Great Lakes, who came aboard as a partner. The ship was christened with his name. When a buyer was not forthcoming, Peck and Hackett formed the Northwestern Transport Company and contracted to carry iron ore from the Jackson Mine in Michigan's Upper Peninsula to the steel mills in Cleveland.

In the spring of 1870, the *Hackett*, under the command of Captain David Trotter, cleared the mouth of the Cuyahoga, steaming on a northwesterly course across Lake Erie toward Detroit trailing a plume of smoke on the first leg of her maiden voyage. Bound for Escanaba on the south shore of Michigan's Upper Peninsula, a powerful compound steam engine with a single screw drove her up to 12 mph (almost 10.5 knots) in the open water. *Hackett* opened her hatches to chutes on the dock at Escanaba. With a thunderous roar, iron ore—nearly twelve hundred tons—filled the ship's holds in a fraction of the time required in the past for teams of dock workers to load vessels manually.

Until this time, a seven-hundred-ton cargo had been considered large. Once loaded and slung low in the water, the *Hackett* steamed east toward the Straits of Mackinac and the lower lakes, headed to deliver her first load of iron ore.

Entering the Straits, she was held up for five hours by "dense fog and a slight accident to her steering gear," according to the May 6 *Detroit Free Press*. Nevertheless, that same article described the voyage as "a very quick trip." Upon her return to Cleveland, critics along the Cuyahoga were silenced. This so-called ugly duckling was a harbinger of things to come, sparking a revolution in Great Lakes shipping.

On May 7, 1870, about the same time the *Hackett* delivered her first cargo, Peck & Masters launched the *Forest City* (216'8" LOA, with a beam of 32'6" and a depth of hold of 13'9") with lines similar to those of the *Hackett*'s, but without an engine. She was initially towed as the *Hackett*'s consort barge—doubling the amount of iron ore that could be shipped at one time. The practice of using consort barges would continue for another twenty years. In

Forest City, built by Peck & Masters, was launched as an engineless tow boat in the spring of 1870. Two years later a compound engine was installed beneath her aft cabin. COURTESY OF THUNDER BAY NATIONAL MARINE SANCTUARY

1872, *Forest City* became a propeller steamer with a new 550-hp compound engine. The *Hackett* caught fire and burned to the waterline on November 12, 1905, at Whaleback Shoal, Lake Michigan, in Green Bay, Wisconsin. Her crew was rescued by the fish tug *Stewart Edward*. The *Forest City*, operating in dense fog in Georgian Bay, on Lake Huron, on May 6, 1904, went aground and was wrecked on Bears Rump Island, near Tobermory, Ontario. Her crew was rescued by the tug *Joe Milton*.

Iron ore is being loaded into the bulk freighter *Alcona* with a dockside steam-shovel bucket. Pocket loading docks with chutes outperformed this method and soon became the industry standard. COURTESY OF THUNDER BAY NATIONAL MARINE SANCTUARY

Eli Peck left shipbuilding in the early 1870s to concentrate on the Northwestern Transport Company, which operated ships in the freight and passenger trades on the Lakes. However, his legacy as a visionary shipbuilder was secure, with more than one hundred vessels to his credit, including the innovative *R. J. Hackett*. Peck died in Detroit on May 8, 1896.

SHIPYARDS AND CONSTRUCTION

Until the late 1880s, Great Lakes shipbuilders clung steadfastly to what they knew best—constructing wooden ships. Although few doubted the future would be in metal ships, the technology was still largely unproven. Two fundamental factors favored wooden shipbuilding: practically priced raw materials (white oak and pine were abundant) and an existing skilled labor force.

In the decade following *Hackett*'s launch, thirty-nine wooden bulk freighters modeled on her design were built. During the 1880s, 143 more wood and steel bulk freighters slid down the ways. These ships doubled in overall length between the early 1870s and the 1890s. Another type of construction, known at the time as "composite construction," featured a wooden hull below the waterline with metal frames and iron or steel topsides. However, shipbuilders soon abandoned this method. Great forethought by canal planners provided for canals that accommodated the ever-increasing size of these ships. The extreme lengths and overall sizes of these new vessels challenged builders. The wooden hulls were stressed near the point of failure when loaded with dense materials like iron ore, coal, grain, and rocks; the demand for increased cargo capacities exacerbated the problem. To counteract this, wooden hull setups were reinforced with iron strapping, which was mortised into the frames in a diagonal, crisscross

The wooden bulk freighter *William B. Morley* (227'2" LOD, 42' beam, 13'11" depth of hold) is shown under construction at Marine City, Michigan, in 1888. COURTESY OF THUNDER BAY NATIONAL MARINE SANCTUARY

configuration. Then, planking was laid over the strapping and frames.

Early bulk carriers, like the *Hackett*, were built with relatively shallow hulls. Because of its extreme weight, iron ore required limited space below decks, but lighter cargoes like coal or grain needed greater capacity to accommodate profitable loads. As a result, later bulk freighters were built with a second (spar) deck above the main deck. Often the lower deck was not planked at all, the deck beams alone providing sufficient reinforcement for the enlarged hulls. The *Hackett* and *Forest City* were both refitted with spar decks in 1881. The *Hackett*'s depth of hold increased from 12'6" to 19'2" and *Forest City*'s from 13'9" to 21'4", creating significantly more cargo space. A strong keel and several keelsons were fundamental to the strength and stiffness of the early wooden bulk freighters, giving them increased longitudinal strength. In addition, this keel assembly acted as a fastening plate for the rest of the framing and was further reinforced by additional timber in the flooring that wasn't incorporated into other types of wooden ships.

Oceanica, launched in 1881 by the Davidson shipyard in West Bay City, Michigan, was the largest vessel sailing the Great Lakes at the time, with a 262'9" LOA, a 37'11" beam, and a 19'11" depth of hold. COURTESY OF THUNDER BAY NATIONAL MARINE SANCTUARY

By the late 1860s, steamers were powered with improved and more powerful steam engines, the result of boilers built with better steel, which permitted higher pressures. Engine technology was ahead of hull technology. Single-cylinder engines were slowly being replaced by compound (two-cylinder) engines. This was more efficient, providing added power for the same amount of fuel. In time, three- and four-cylinder engines were developed, further enhancing efficiency and power.

Captain James E. Davidson, a prominent wooden ship builder, set up operations along the Saginaw River in West Bay City (known today as Bay City), Michigan, in 1871. Over the next thirty-two years, his yard built the largest wooden ships on the Great Lakes. Born in Buffalo, New York, in 1841, Davidson sailed the Great Lakes and earned his master's papers at the age of nineteen. He spent two years on the oceans in his early twenties, before returning to the Lakes as a ship's master and eventually becoming an owner.

Davidson worked in shipyards at Buffalo and Toledo, learning the trade before settling in West Bay City. There he built a sawmill, which was a new concept in shipbuilding at that time. In 1873, the keel was laid for the yard's first steam-powered bulk freighter, the *James Davidson*—230'7" LOA, 37' beam, and 19'7" depth of hold—which was more than 20' longer than the *R. J. Hackett*. Along with becoming famous for her size, the *Davidson* gained notoriety as the first ship on the Lakes built with timbers cut in a shipyard sawmill. A shipyard fire severely damaged the *Davidson* while she was still on the stocks, but she was rebuilt and entered service on June 23, 1874. On September 12, she cleared Chicago with 60,700 bushels of grain. A month later, she carried 110,000 bushels of oats to Buffalo. Unfortunately, the *Davidson*, sailing from Buffalo to Duluth, Minnesota, with her consort barge *Middlesex*, struck the southeast end of Thunder Bay Island thirteen miles off Alpena, Michigan, in Lake Huron, and was lost on April 10, 1883.

As a result of the economic downturn which had started in 1873, Davidson was forced to close down the yard. However, by 1880, the shipyard was again in operation. The steamship *Oceanica*, then the largest ship on the lakes (262'9" LOA,

Tampa **strained the size limits of wooden bulk freighters (see line drawing on page 78). She sailed the Great Lakes until 1911, when she sank following a collision with the freighter** *John W. Gates* **in the Detroit River.** COURTESY OF THUNDER BAY NATIONAL MARINE SANCTUARY

with a beam of 37'11" and a 19'11" depth of hold) was launched in 1881 and entered service on August 17 of that year. *Oceanica* carried grain and lumber on the Lakes until 1919 when she burned on the St. Lawrence River.

Captain Frank W. Wheeler established a shipyard along the Saginaw River in West Bay City in 1876. In 1890, the enormous bulk freighter *Tampa*—291'7" LOA, with a beam of 41' and a 19'10" depth of hold—slid down the ways into the Saginaw. The *Tampa*, driven by a 1,000-hp steam engine, sailed in the Great Lakes trade carrying iron ore and coal until July 18, 1911, when she collided with the freighter *John W. Gates* in the Detroit

River at Walkerville, Ontario. At nearly 300' LOA, *Tampa* was approaching the maximum length for a wooden bulk carrier. In 1900, Wheeler sold the business to The American Ship Building Company.

A wooden freighter launched in Milwaukee, Wisconsin, by the Wolf & Davidson yard in 1888 as the *George H. Dyer*—208'10" LOA, with a beam of 35'1" and a 21'7" depth of hold—quietly established her place in Great Lakes maritime history in 1902. After carrying bulk cargoes for nearly fourteen seasons, she was renamed *Hennepin* in 1898. Four years later, the steamer was fitted with an elevator belt and is believed to have been the first self-unloader in the world. In her twilight years, *Hennepin* played out her career as a towed barge. On August 18, 1927, she foundered while under tow and sank off South Haven, Michigan.

Through the 1890s and into the early years of the twentieth century, wooden bulk freighters continued as workhorses on the Great Lakes—but their days were numbered. The last of the wooden bulk carriers were built in 1902, stretching to 310' LOA, soon to be displaced by steel freighters that had by then far surpassed their wooden sisters in size and capability. The steel ship *Victory* (400' LOA) was launched in 1894, followed by the *John W. Gates* (500' LOA) in 1900, and by several six-hundred-footers just six years later. Nearly a century and a half after Eli Peck launched his revolutionary *R. J. Hackett*, modern bulk carriers—many stretching to 1,000' LOA—sail the same routes as their wooden predecessors, a fitting legacy for the first long ships that sailed the Great Lakes.

THE IRON ORE TRADE ON THE GREAT LAKES

Iron ore was discovered in Michigan's Upper Peninsula on September 19, 1844, by a geological survey party led by William A. Burt, a US deputy surveyor. The find on the rugged Marquette Range influenced the development of shipping and commercial trade on the Great Lakes for nearly 150 years. The Jackson Mine, established in 1845 at the site of present-day Negaunee, Michigan, was the first to operate on the iron range. Present-day Marquette, established in 1849, is located fourteen miles east-northeast of the mine and had the closest natural harbor on Lake Superior's south shore. Marquette—or "Iron Bay," as settlers called it—was the first port to ship iron ore on the Great Lakes.

Mining companies planned to forge raw ore into iron bars—or blooms—four inches square and two feet in length to transport them to Iron Bay and load them aboard ships bound for steel mills on the lower lakes in Ohio and Pennsylvania. The entire process was cumbersome and expensive. At Sault Ste. Marie, Michigan, on the eastern shore of Lake Superior, ships were unloaded, their cargo portaged past falls on the St. Mary's River and reloaded aboard other vessels for the run down the lakes. The original iron ore carriers were general-purpose schooners or steamers, both side-wheelers, and propellers, so designated because of their propulsion. During the early 1850s, there were only three or four schooners and even fewer small steamers sailing on Lake Superior.

By 1853, mining companies scrapped the idea of shipping iron blooms in favor of raw iron ore, which was hauled from the mines to a small dock on Iron Bay by wagons (sleighs in winter) drawn by teams of oxen,

Elevated pocket ore docks at Marquette, Michigan, changed the iron ore industry, allowing iron ore to slide down chutes into the holds of vessels, a process once done by wallopers with wheelbarrows and shovels. Notice the photographer's shadow in the foreground. COURTESY OF SUPERIOR VIEW IN MARQUETTE, MICHIGAN

mules, or horses. Workmen, known as "dock-wallopers," hand-loaded ore aboard ships with wheelbarrows. In 1855, thirty men were needed to load a three-hundred-ton cargo, which was a common-sized shipment. It would take them six days.

Construction of a canal around the falls at Sault Ste. Marie was completed on June 18, 1855. The canal, known today as the Soo Locks, opened the flow of upbound and downbound traffic between Lake Superior and the four other Great Lakes. On August 17, the brig *Columbia* cleared Lighthouse Point at Marquette bound for Sault Ste. Marie and secured her

Railroad cars dumped iron ore into pocket docks, and then workmen, called "dock-wallopers," shoveled excess ore into the pockets (bins). Chutes below would then direct ore into the holds of bulk freighters, barges, and schooners.
COURTESY OF SUPERIOR VIEW IN MARQUETTE, MICHIGAN

place in history as the first ship to carry iron ore through the canal.

Marquette made history in 1857 when the world's first elevated pocket loading dock was completed, allowing iron ore to slide down chutes into the holds of vessels, eliminating the need for wallopers to walk loads aboard in wheelbarrows. Pockets (large holding bins) on the docks stored ore until ships were in place for loading. As the iron ore industry matured, pocket docks became standard at other Lake Superior ports (Duluth and Two Harbors, Minnesota; Superior and Ashland, Wisconsin; L'Anse, Michigan; and Thunder Bay, Ontario). On Lake Michigan, Escanaba and Gladstone, Michigan, became iron ore ports, as did St. Ignace, Michigan, and Little Current, Ontario.

In the mid-1850s, a railroad line connected the Jackson Mine with the docks in Marquette Harbor. In the years ahead, railroad lines across the iron ranges would prove to be paramount in increasing the efficiency of transporting ore to the shores, significantly advancing the expansion and development of the iron ore trade.

During the American Civil War, Union soldiers were supplied with cannons and guns formed from iron ore that was mined on the northern ranges. Trains hauling passengers and goods across the northern United States during the second half of the nineteenth century rolled on rails made from that same ore.

As the wooden-hulled bulk freighter *R. J. Hackett* sailed north to collect her first iron ore cargo from the Jackson Mine in the spring of 1870, the industry's infrastructure—pocket docks, the Soo Locks, and railroad lines—was now in place in more strategic locations. By 1888, iron ore was the dominant trade on the Great Lakes, supplanting grain and lumber.

Although the iron ore trade has passed its peak, steel-hulled bulk freighters up to 1,000' LOA—commonly called ore boats—continue to ply the waters of the Great Lakes, slipping quietly into harbors still operating docks, filling their holds, and sailing for mills down the Lakes just as their wooden predecessors did over a century ago.

LAKE SUPERIOR'S SHIPWRECK COAST

Mariners have long respected—if not feared—the Lake Superior shoreline between Munising and Whitefish Point in Michigan's Upper Peninsula. Called the "Shipwreck Coast," the eighty-mile stretch has no natural harbors. Whitefish Point, which juts northeast toward the Canadian border just four miles away, has been a perilous crossroads for upbound and downbound bulk freighters for nearly 150 years.

It is estimated that there are as many as 150 shipwrecks near Whitefish Point, victims of prevailing northwest winds, steep seas, dense fog, blinding snow squalls, smoke from occasional forest fires, and considerable traffic during the shipping season. The average water depth is 150 feet, though in spots, it plunges to 400 feet.

Among the wrecks are five vessels—steam-powered, propeller-driven bulk freighters—offering a window into the life and times of the ships that opened trade routes for the iron mines in Michigan and Minnesota, the coal fields of Ohio, and the grain fields across America's Heartland. Each of the ships sunk after a collision, is still relatively intact, and provides an example of change in bulk freighter design from the earliest vessels, which began in 1869 with the launch of Elihu M. Peck's *R. J. Hackett.*

The Great Lakes Shipwreck Historical Society—under project director Thomas L. Farnquist, with principal investigator Patrick Labadie—launched an underwater archaeological project in 2003 to assess and document five bulk freighter wrecks near Whitefish Point. The intent was to photograph and gather information to share with current generations about

This watercolor by Robert McGreevy shows the propeller *Vienna* (194'5" LOA, 33'10" beam, and 14'1" draft) passing the Whitefish Point Light Station in 1892 (courtesy Great Lakes Shipwreck Museum). Built in 1887 at Cleveland, Ohio, in the Quayle and Martin Shipyards, she sunk off Whitefish Point on September 19, 1892, after colliding with the freighter *Nipigon.*
© ROBERT MCGREEVY

shipbuilding, the perils of navigating Lake Superior, and the significance of Great Lakes commerce. Additionally, the project team planned to identify threats to the wreck sites and monitor their changes over time. The spread of zebra mussels in the Lower Great Lakes added urgency to the task.

Among the five bulk freighter wrecks were four wooden vessels:

- *Comet* (181'2" LOA, a 29' beam, and a 13'3" depth of hold) was built in 1857 as a passenger and package freight vessel and later reconstructed as a prototypical bulk carrier, sunk in an 1875 collision.
- *Vienna* (194'5" LOA, a 33'10" beam, and a 14'1" depth) was built in 1887 and wrecked in 1892.
- *John M. Osborne* (196' LOA, a 32'1" beam, and a 14' depth) was built in 1882 and wrecked in 1884.
- *Samuel Mather* (254' LOA, a 40'1" beam, and a 19'4" depth) was built in 1887 and wrecked in 1891.
- *John B. Cowle*, a steel bulk freighter built in 1902 (420' LOA, a 50'2" beam, and a 24' depth), was also studied and compared with her wooden predecessors.

At the project's finish, Pat Labadie concluded that the five vessels illuminate "the genius of shipbuilders who responded to the economic and industrial incentives of their era and developed specialized, efficient ships to transport the requisite commodities."

By preserving the five vessels in the cold depths of Lake Superior, the Shipwreck Coast—in an ironic twist—has provided new generations with a view into the past. Had these vessels survived their collisions, likely their remnants wouldn't exist today.

RECREATION, A ROGUE, AND A LEGENDARY GREAT LAKES HISTORIAN

Heavily laden with gear, the 30' launch *Abbie* voyaged seven hundred miles in western Lake Superior under skipper John Munro Longyear and his crew of six friends, seen here with netting protecting their faces and necks against bites by the ubiquitous mosquitoes and blackflies. The trek was very likely the first recreational powerboat voyage on the lake.

CHAPTER 5

Cruise of the *Abbie*

AN 1889 LAKE SUPERIOR ADVENTURE

On a midsummer's morning in 1889, a zephyr rippled across the harbor in Marquette, Michigan, stirring the long skirts of ladies on the dock, and the Stars and Stripes flying on a stern staff stepped on the fantail of the launch *Abbie*. The diminutive craft—30' LOA, with a 5'6" beam, a draft of 21"—was about to embark on a month's coastal cruise around Lake Superior with a six-man crew, including owner John Munro Longyear.

The sleek launch, propelled by a 4-hp naphtha engine (see sidebar, page 111), was the latest thing for amateur motorboaters. She was capable of reaching 6 mph in quiet waters. *Abbie*'s white, carvel-planked hull was packed to the gunwales with provisions and gear. Between her 5'-long foredeck and 4'-long after deck, the cockpit was open. The engine was mounted well aft, as in all naphtha launches, and had a signature burnished brass boiler and integral stack. A seventy-gallon fuel tank was fitted under the foredeck, and amidships a one-hundred-gallon drum containing additional fuel was mounted on blocks. Bench seats extended 17' along each side, with one thwart in the bow and another forward of the engine. The white oak, ash, cedar, and mahogany of the gunwales, coaming, decks, and inside trim were finished with shellac. Small sprit-rigged sails could be raised on each mast—one far forward and the other abaft the spare naphtha drum. These provided alternative power in favorable conditions and stabilized the boat in a blow. A pair of ruby-striped canvas

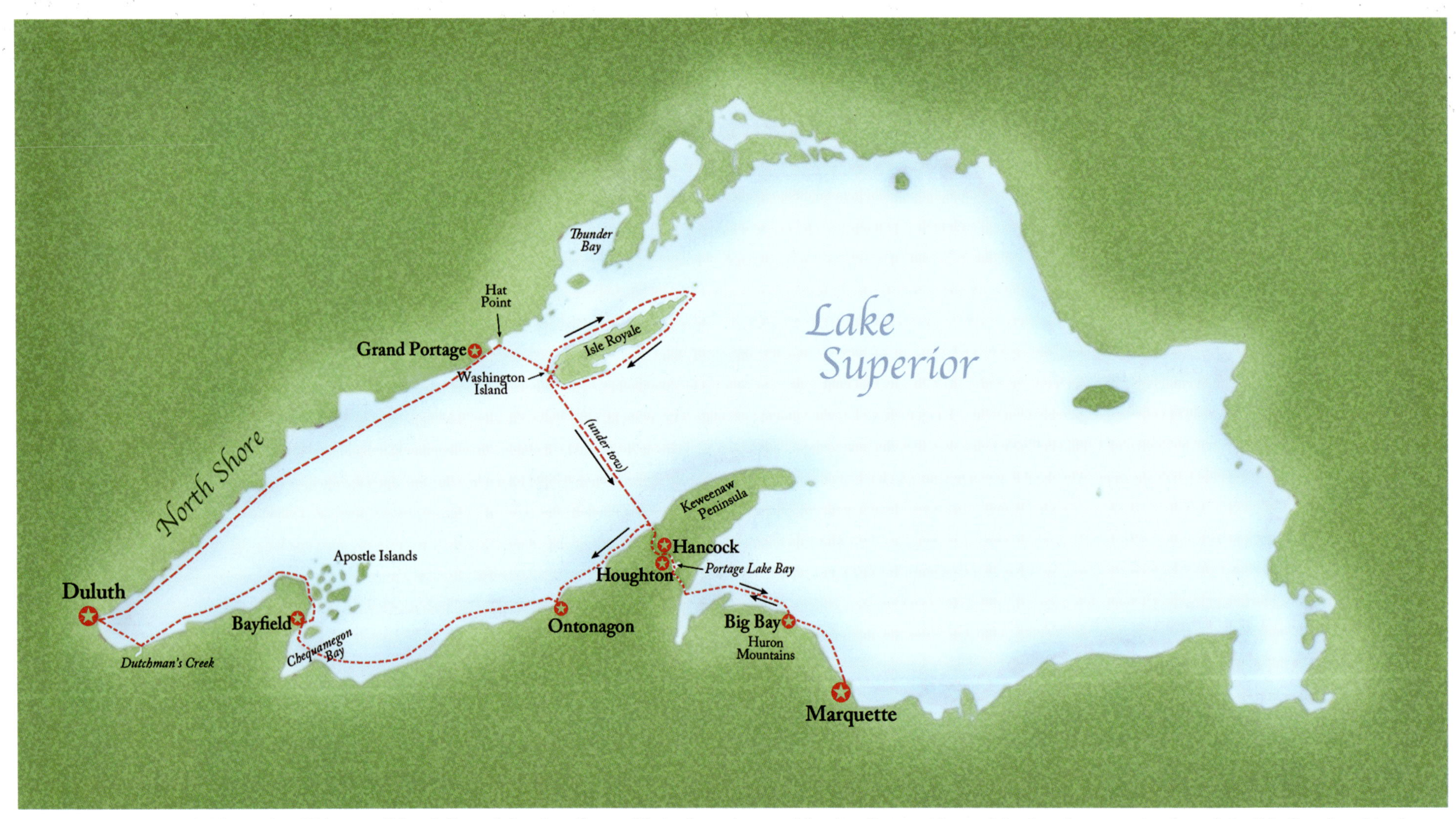

Leaving Marquette, Michigan, the *Abbie* expedition followed the shorelines of Lake Superior, reaching its climax with an eight-day circumnavigation of the Isle Royal archipelago. A tow from a steamer thence to the Keweenaw Peninsula hastened the return and spared the crew a long open-water crossing. MAP BY *WOODENBOAT* Magazine

awnings—a flat one for a sunshade and a peaked one for wet weather—could be folded or rolled for easy stowage. The crew took their meals at a table that could be knocked down for stowage.

Other than a sendoff from a few well-wishers, there was little fanfare as the hands stepped aboard. At precisely 10:45, Longyear ordered the mooring lines cast off and the engine engaged. Final farewells were shouted as the sleek craft cleared the dock and gained headway toward the south end of the breakwater and the open lake. *Abbie*—named for Longyear's daughter, Abby, though spelled differently—was outward bound on a journey that would cover nearly seven hundred miles. Longyear believed she was the first recreational motorboat on Lake Superior. Up until *Abbie*'s arrival, schooners, bulk freighters, passenger steamers, Mackinaw boats, and canoes had dominated the world's largest freshwater lake.

NAPTHA ENGINES AND LAUNCHES

Gas Engine & Power Company in Morris Heights, New York City, began manufacturing naphtha engines and launches along the Harlem River

Abby Longyear. MARQUETTE REGIONAL HISTORY CENTER

in 1886. Autumn leaves were falling that October when Longyear (see sidebar, page 109) visited the plant to look at the new boats. Obviously impressed, he ordered a 30' model the following March. "I care more for strength and utility than for ornament," he wrote in a letter to the company. "It will frequently be necessary in my cruising about the great lakes [*sic*] to draw the boat out on the beach. She should therefore be rigged with a strongly anchored ring in her stem to which tackle blocks may be attached and she should also be so strongly built that she will not be racked by being frequently beached."

Abbie was finished by mid-May. Longyear and three companions, including his brother Howard, traveled to New York by railroad before the end of the month to take possession. Rather than shipping the boat by train to Marquette, he planned to run her up the Hudson River, through the Erie Canal, into the Great Lakes, and ultimately to her home port on the south shore of Lake Superior. After being launched in the Harlem River, *Abbie* passed into the Hudson River and headed north.

Avid sportsmen and anglers, the crew often tried their luck for trout and pike, which were plentiful in what was still very much a wilderness. MARQUETTE REGIONAL HISTORY CENTER

The journey ended unexpectedly in Albany, New York, however, when a telegram summoned Longyear to Ashland, Wisconsin, on important business. *Abbie* completed her maiden voyage aboard a flatcar.

Lake Superior was still very much a wilderness at that time, and over the ensuing two summers, Longyear cruised its rugged coastline and sugar-sand beaches within fifty miles of Marquette.

Describing this period in his memoirs, he recalled: "fishing for large speckled-trout on the reefs and wherever large broken rocks could be found on or near the shore." He and a group of cronies were eager to extend *Abbie's* range with an expedition that would follow the shoreline west and north, and by 1889 they were ready. The long-awaited day came on Monday, July 22.

NORTHWARD BOUND

After rounding the head of the breakwater in Marquette harbor, *Abbie* headed north, leaving to port the prominent yellow-brick, story-and-a-half, forty-foot-tall, square lighthouse with its fourth-order Fresnel lens. The crew was a patchwork of characters, including two physicians, an engineer, a Norwegian sailor, a banker, and Longyear. An accomplished writer despite his limited formal education, Longyear kept a detailed journal during the cruise. He also documented events with his Kodak camera.

As civilization slowly receded in *Abbie's* wake, the crew set about loosely organizing themselves. One physician was appointed "surgeon" and the other

Abbie was packed with gear for the month of voyaging, including two small sprit sails that could be set when the wind was favorable. MARQUETTE REGIONAL HISTORY CENTER

"steward." The engineer naturally took responsibility for operating and maintaining the engine. The Norwegian sailor, called "Mox" by the crew, was assigned several titles, among them cook, able seaman, and "crew of the captain's gig," the small skiff towed along as a means for reaching shore when they could not beach the launch. Longyear himself, called the "bushwhacker" for unknown reasons, was named "captain." The banker, whose "nautical experience was confined to cruising in a flat-bottomed skiff on a millpond . . . was a problem until one of the crew in a moment of inspiration nominated him for chaplain, and he was immediately elected by acclamation. And a very good chaplain he made—not too severe in dealing with the erring mortals composing the crew. . . ."

Abbie pushed through the swells off Presque Isle, once a Native American settlement, "with its cliffs of banded red and white sandstone." Passing a cave, the captain suspended election proceedings to point out favored fishing spots among the black rocks, including where "the big one got away!" Others piped up with similar tales, causing the steward to suggest stowing fish stories for the duration. Finally, approaching a beautiful, lush-green archipelago overlooked by Sugarloaf, the most easterly of the Huron Mountains, a hungry crew consumed a meager meal prepared by the steward and Mox.

A MAGNIFICENT PANORAMA

Cutting across Big Bay late that afternoon, the Huron Mountains, backlit by the sun, spilled purple shadows in diminishing hues into the valleys below, while peaks were flooded with radiant rays, illuminating "shades of green foliage . . . except where an occasional granite cliff rears its barren head above the sea of verdure." Spread before them was a magnificent panorama of natural beauty, which they savored with each passing day. As *Abbie* closed with the southwest corner of the bay, a settlement consisting of small log huts was visible on the shore. Among the fishermen who were there were several Indians, "looked at with much interest by some of the crew whose acquaintance with the fast-disappearing aborigines was limited," especially the engineer, who had never seen Indians before. After a brief respite on shore, *Abbie* headed north again, seeking the low sand dunes at the mouth of the Pine River, where the group planned to set up camp for the night.

Upon reaching the Pine, the launch ran "into the center of the narrow, coffee-colored current flowing into the clear water of the lake . . . the

With few exceptions, the *Abbie* voyagers spent nights ashore, as here at their Pine River tent encampment on July 23, their second night out. MARQUETTE REGIONAL HISTORY CENTER

crew set up camp on the upper part of a wide beach, "where the heavy seas of last autumn's gales had leveled it." The tent, blankets, canvas cots, oil cookstove, and food were ferried ashore in the skiff. The crew soon learned they were not alone. A fishing party from Houghton—sailing a Mackinaw boat—was camped farther upstream, and an Indian family traveling by bark canoe from L'Anse was in the vicinity, harvesting birch bark. Although scarce, traffic on the lake along the undeveloped shore included an occasional packet steamer trailing smoke from her stack and carrying freight and passengers between Duluth, Minnesota, and the Lower Great Lakes.

The crew bedded down in the tent, with the exception of Mox, who slept soundly aboard *Abbie* until 3:00 a.m., when "a swell, rolling in from the lake pitched the launch about." At 6:00 a.m., the others awoke to the strong aroma of ham sizzling on the cookstove, as Mox, now wide awake, prepared breakfast in the fresh morning air. During the meal, "the captain amused himself by taking kodak [*sic*] photographs of the members of the

engine checked down to sufficient speed for 'steerage-way' only." Although Longyear had been assured by fishermen at Big Bay that the Pine was deep enough for *Abbie*, the captain had good reason to be cautious. Sandbars stretched across the river, and the launch grounded on one but sustained no damage. Rather than entering the river, the captain decided to anchor *Abbie* offshore. The

crew in unconscious attitudes." By 8:45 a.m., with the camp dismantled and gear stowed aboard *Abbie*, the cruise continued westward.

To port, vertical cliffs with red sandstone-carved arches and pillars, accented the rugged coastline between bronze beaches leading inland to virgin forests. To starboard, the vast lake—in its many moods, with shades of blue and gray, depending on cloud cover—reached the far horizon. The crisp, clear, shoal waters near shore were often too inviting for the fishermen aboard, who were eager "to stop and 'wet a line.'" Fishing, a favorite recreation, was also a practical means of stocking the larder.

SUPERIOR'S OPEN WATERS

As the voyage continued to the west and north, "the Abbies," as they came to be known, encountered Mackinaw boats with Indian crews, among whom the launch and its brass stack elicited stares of surprise and wonder. Chippewa bands for three centuries had lived off the forests and the "Big-Sea-Water" celebrated in Henry Wadsworth Longfellow's *The Song of Hiawatha*, and they were

Abbie, with her awning rigged, prepared to venture north through the Portage River, a partly natural, partly dredged waterway bisecting the Keeweenaw Peninsula. MARQUETTE REGIONAL HISTORY CENTER

reluctantly sharing nature's bounty and the lake that had once been theirs alone.

Conditions dictated the prevailing spirit of the crew. As *Abbie* crossed the Keweenaw Peninsula via the Portage River, Portage Lake, and the Keweenaw ship canal, the "persistent buzzing songs of the first mosquitoes" intruded on a shoreside supper. Thick fog and heavy dew greeted the Abbies on some mornings, meaning they had to stow the tent aboard while it was still wet. On Superior's open waters southwest of the Keeweenaw, black clouds announced the coming of a squall, and seas built as the crew struck sail, rigged the canvas cover over the cockpit, and donned foul weather gear, even as sheets of rain swept over the launch. On wet days, the burner under the engine's boiler was the only dry spot in the boat. Despite avalanches of water, the little engine purred steadily along, with the blue-gas naphtha flame maintaining a gentle roar.

A fire ashore was an absolute necessity at day's end to warm and cheer the weary mariners. The fire dried their tent canvas and their soaked clothing. Driftwood piled high on beaches—a gift of the previous autumn's gales—provided abundant fuel, seating, and places to hang gear to dry. Lake Superior's storms were a constant threat, with conditions often shifting rapidly from dead calm to a violent tempest, followed by relative calm again. Cruising southwest of Ontonagon, Michigan, *Abbie* was close to shore when a strong wind, "a furious wild beast," roared out of the northwest, bringing with it "a purple darkness and an opaque sheet of descending water." Buckets of hail came next, causing a terrific "din and racket" with "an

inspirational, grand cadence in it not at all unmusical." Twigs, leaves, and branches torn from trees filled the air near the beach as the launch ran along in calm waters under the lee of a headland. A hundred yards farther out, "the lake was milky-white with foam and spray torn from the surging [seas] and hurled about in white sheets and jets often fifty feet in height." The violence ended within minutes, and in steady rain, *Abbie* and her crew steered to an anchorage, pitched the wet tent, and settled in with a large driftwood fire near its opening to play a card game called Crazy Pedro.

EXPLORATION ISLAND

Exploring inland on foot or rowing the skiff up rivers revealed more of the pristine natural charm of the virtually untouched wilderness. The captain and his companions were captivated by cascading waterfalls, rushing rapids, high red-clay banks alternating with sand-rock cliffs, and deep ravines with small streams flowing into larger rivers. Up-close-and-personal encounters with wildlife—including gray wolves, which the crew did not consider dangerous—were common. The crew thought of the cuts, bruises, and strained muscles they suffered while stumbling over the rough terrain as small prices to pay for their experiences. Occasional skinny-dipping in crisp river waters was a refreshing treat and sharpened appetites.

The elements also battered *Abbie*. A mysterious hull leak was finally revealed when the launch was suspended with a block-and-tackle from a tree limb overhanging the Black River. Two large screws securing the stern bearing were at fault. One was broken, and the other loosened, allowing the sleeve to shift position and the leak to form. With repairs made and the naphtha burner lit, the launch was soon underway, bound for the Wisconsin and Minnesota shores curving around the western end of Superior.

On August 9, 1889, *Abbie*, with her ruby-striped awning set up for foul weather, put into cross river, on Minnesota's rocky, and then quite remote, North Shore, adjacent to a fisherman's cabin. MARQUETTE REGIONAL HISTORY CENTER

As *Abbie* crossed the northern end of Chequamegon Bay on a northwesterly course for Bayfield, Wisconsin, "the seas encountered were high, steep, and running swiftly," and threatened to swamp the launch. Nevertheless, *Abbie* was non-plussed, "cleaving the green wall with her cutwater . . . in a shower of white spray." At Bayfield, the launch landed at the main steamer dock, allowing the crew to procure provisions and newspapers, as well as inquire about mail, and "to generally rub up against civilization again for an hour or two."

Duluth was the next port of call. Camping twelve miles south of the city at Dutchman's Creek, the Abbies were captivated after dark by "the electric lights of Duluth on the hillsides like an enormous torch-light parade . . . reflected in the gently undulating, glassy surface of the lake . . . a brilliant dancing, luminous track across the water, reaching almost to our feet." The next day *Abbie* lay at a wharf in the city, loading supplies, while a crowd gathered to speculate about the unusual craft. "Where does she carry the fuel?" one mused. Another suggested, "It's a guv'ment boat!" A boy exclaimed to his pal, "Tommy, she's a grocery boat!" By late afternoon, the launch was underway along Minnesota's picturesque, rocky North Shore, with its lovely small bays and natural harbors.

Passing Grand Portage, once a major depot for fur traders and voyageurs, "the hills of Isle Royale slowly rose higher and higher, in azure billows" off *Abbie*'s port bow. Turning toward the island at Hat Point, the launch moved through smooth waters until encountering a southeast breeze, when "the foresail was raised and the exhilarating ride across the broad expanse of heaving water was heartily appreciated by the crew." Starting at Washington Island in the southwest and following a clockwise route for eight days, *Abbie* circumnavigated the archipelago consisting of Isle Royale, surrounded by over 450 smaller islands. Returning to Washington Harbor, *Abbie*'s inventory was in frightful shape, "a burned and dilapidated tent; mouldy bread; supplies nearly gone; naphtha getting low; the raiment and personal appearance of the crew very much the worse for wear."

No longer enthralled with roughing it, the crew loaded *Abbie*'s gear and skiff aboard the steamer *A. B. Taylor*, and with the launch in tow, the captain and his crew enjoyed a brief respite while en route south across the lake to Hancock, on the Keweenaw Peninsula's ship canal, only a two-day voyage from home. Mox elected to stay aboard *Abbie* for the crossing and later "acknowledged that, after having sailed the world over, he had just had the wildest boat-ride of his life. . . ." After replenishing the larder in nearby Houghton, the launch resumed her voyage, continuing through the ship canal and then turning east toward Marquette.

HOMEWARD BOUND

With seas running too briskly to chance a landing in Big Bay, the crew, now craving the comforts of home, bedded down for its final night aboard the launch. At 5:15 the following morning, *Abbie*'s crew started the dependable naphtha engine and raised the sails. The launch surged southeast, with the main and foresail full and the screw turning,

driving *Abbie* homeward. Leaving Lighthouse Point to starboard and rounding the Marquette breakwater, *Abbie*, "with sails set and colors flying, glided alongside and stopped at the landing from which she had been absent just thirty days." In that time, the launch covered more than seven hundred miles. Writing later, Longyear recalled, "The trip was a notable achievement at that time and was considered reckless by many who were not accustomed to cruising. It was perfectly safe, or as safe as any boat on large bodies of water and was thoroughly enjoyed by the party."

By the early 1900s, with the arrival of gasoline engines, naphtha launches like *Abbie* had become relics, as had the earlier steam launches. But in her time, she shimmered in the sun, leaving an indelible mark on the region's maritime history as, in all likelihood, the first recreational powerboat on Lake Superior.

JOHN MUNRO LONGYEAR

John Munro Longyear arrived in Marquette, Michigan, aboard the wooden propeller steamer *Rocket* as a sharp-featured twenty-three-year-old with a dark, full beard and mustache. Born near Lansing, Michigan, in 1850, he ended his formal education at age fifteen because of health problems, and before arriving in Marquette, he had held a variety of jobs, including store clerk, post office clerk, law clerk, deputy US marshal, and a lumber mill log scaler. Moving north, however, he found his true calling. With little money in his pocket when he stepped ashore, he sought to advance his career by becoming a "land looker," exploring Michigan's Upper Peninsula wilderness to assess, purchase, and sell lands rich in minerals and timber. It was the foundation of a career that lasted more than fifty years, during which he amassed a fortune.

Longyear proved his mettle during the Panic of 1873, weathering the five-year worldwide financial storm. Carrying an eighty-pound rucksack, he trekked deep into the north woods, accompanied by Indian guides and fellow lookers. Living in the wild for weeks at a time, he assessed and mapped the land and natural resources for clients, who often paid him in acreage rather than money. Late in life, Longyear acknowledged the role outdoor living had played in his personal development. Within twenty-four hours of returning to town, he once wrote, "I was eager to return to outdoor living, which tended to develop a man's self-reliance, patience, and perseverance, in fact, all his physical and mental resources. You are obliged to do everything on your own."

John Munro Longyear. MARQUETTE REGIONAL HISTORY CENTER

By 1878, the slender explorer was a seasoned and respected land looker. A year later, he married Marquette schoolteacher Mary Hawley Beecher. Longyear continued to build the business while Mary looked after the household and, eventually, their six children. Already a wealthy man by the mid-1880s, Longyear secured his fortune with an agreement to develop iron ore in Minnesota's rich Mesabi Range.

Over the years, Longyear owned a variety of small boats, one of them being the naphtha launch *Abbie*. His business interests also extended to Lake Superior. During the 1890s, he operated a steam propeller service between Marquette and Houghton on the Keweenaw Peninsula, sixty miles to the northwest, with the 94' *City of New Baltimore* and later the 114'2" *City of Marquette*. In 1892, Longyear was among the founders of the Huron Mountain Shooting and Fishing Club, located on a vast and remote tract of primeval forest northwest of Big Bay, Michigan. Restricted to one hundred members, the club, which continues today as the Huron Mountain Club, was so exclusive that even automobile pioneer Henry Ford had to wait thirteen years for admittance.

Early in the twentieth century, Longyear looked outside the United States for potential land and natural resources. He established the Arctic Coal Company to survey and mine coal deposits on Spitsbergen Island (now Svalbard) off northwestern Norway between 1905 and 1916. The company, headquartered in Boston, created Longyear City, population of five hundred. The name survives today as Longyearbyen. Longyear died in Brookline, Massachusetts, in 1922.

NAPHTHA LAUNCHES

Swedish immigrant Frank M. Ofeldt patented his revolutionary naphtha engine design in 1883. And two years later, he was building the first boats to put them to use, signaling a new era in marine propulsion. The engines were a clear alternative to steam power for avocational boaters. At that time, the United States required every steam-driven watercraft, private or commercial, to have a licensed engineer aboard to avoid the common problem of boiler explosion.

Naphtha engines didn't fall under the rule, so anyone for whom it was impractical to become licensed quickly adopted them. The engines were also much lighter: a 2-hp naphtha engine weighed only two hundred pounds, compared to the one thousand pounds of its steam-powered counterpart.

Ofeldt's design used a flash boiler mounted over an enclosed three-cylinder engine. The boiler vaporized naphtha that was hand-pumped from a fuel tank.

Naphtha launches, shown in this advertisement, were a singular success, with more than four thousand built in its first ten years. The naphtha engines bridged the gap between steam engines and gasoline-powered motors introduced in 1900.

At the base of the boiler, the labeled port "A" is the sight hole allowing inspection of the flame. To the left, "B" marks the hand air-pump used to pressurize the fuel tank.

The naphtha expanded in the engine valve chest to drive the pistons with greater power than steam could achieve at the same pressure. The small amount of vapor drawn off through an injector to feed the burner was the only expenditure of fuel, with the exhaust venting through the brass stack. The bulk of the naphtha circulated over and over through the vaporization and condensing phases, with exhaust gases flowing through water-cooled condenser tubes outside the hull, returning as a liquid to the fuel tank.

Starting a naphtha engine was a straightforward process. Controls were mounted on a thwart forward of the engine. The operator used a hand pump to pressurize the fuel tank, forcing vapor into a circular burner under the boiler coils. The vapor was ignited with a match thrust through a touch-hole. Once the coils were sufficiently heated, a naphtha pump forced cold liquid naphtha into them, building pressure. As the pressure reached ten to fifteen pounds, an injector valve was opened to mix vapor with air to fuel the burner. At twenty pounds pressure, a hand wheel was turned to open slide valves, driving the pistons and turning the propeller. The engine could be reversed by firmly twisting the hand wheel—even at top speed. To stop, the operator closed the injector valve to extinguish the fire and secured the hand wheel. At the time these engines entered the market, naphtha, a by-product of petroleum distillation, was typically thrown away. However, Standard Oil Company, believing in the clear liquid's potential as a fuel, partially funded the start-up of the Gas Engine & Power Company in 1886 to manufacture naphtha engines and launches. By 1889, the company was building boats

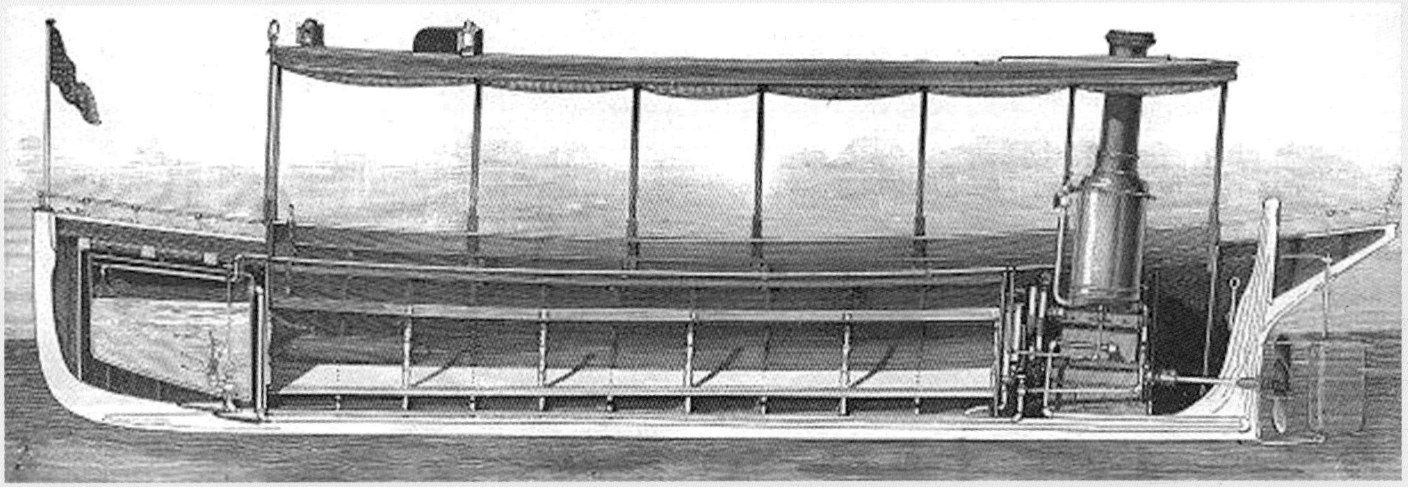

In a naphtha launch, the fuel tank installed well forward balanced the engine mounted well aft, allowing a large, open central cockpit. A pipe carried fuel from the tank to be vaporized and mixed with air to fuel the boiler. Unused naphtha was recondensed and returned to the fuel tank by a separate pipe. AUTHOR'S COLLECTION

from 18' to 75' long, powered by engines of 1 to 16 hp to speeds of between 7 and 11 mph.

The designs of these sleek boats varied little. They had plumb stems, moderate deadrise amidships, moderate sheer, fantail sterns, and either lapstrake or carvel white cedar planking over hackmatack frames and white oak keels. Bench seats ran along each side. Small launches were open or had canopies with curtains, and sometimes they were fitted with a vertical tiller on the thwart forward of the engine or a tiller rope running under the coaming outboard of the seats. Some large models had cabins, often with a raised helm station, while others had steering wheels mounted on a forward bulkhead. The lightweight engines, which were manufactured to have interchangeable parts, sat in brass-lined wells at the stern and had integral brass stacks, and the fuel tank was placed at the bow. This arrangement allowed for ample cockpit space in contrast to steam launches, in which the heavy engines and boilers were placed amidships.

The new launches were a singular success. Gas Engine & Power built more than four thousand in its first ten years. The boats eventually reached ports throughout the United States and in Europe, South America, India, and as far away as Hawaii. They were popular as resort launches, and schooners and steam yachts frequently carried small naphtha tenders on davits. Naphtha engines bridged the gap between steam engines and the introduction in 1900 of gasoline-powered motors, known initially as "explosive engines." The popularity of naphtha engines and launches, which could not compete with the power and convenience of boats with gasoline engines, faded early in the twentieth century.

Various stages in building their high-quality craft were constantly in motion in the Truscott boat construction shop. Twenty-six launches 16' to 50' are visible in this photograph.
HERITAGE MUSEUM AND CULTURAL CENTER, ST. JOSEPH, MICHIGAN

Truscott Boat Manufacturing Company

A SHINING STAR OF AMERICAN INDUSTRY

America was sliding into the abyss of an economic depression in 1892, but boatbuilder Thomas Henry Truscott—a visionary in the spirit of Henry Ford—imagined a shining future for recreational watercraft in America. Despite the nation's financial woes, which would culminate with the Panic of 1893 (which set off a depression that lasted until 1897), Truscott envisioned a prosperous future for the company he managed with his sons—John, James, and Edward. Born in 1826, Thomas Truscott began his career as an apprentice under his uncle, a master boatbuilder, in Falmouth, England, on the rugged Cornish coast. By the time Truscott Boat Manufacturing Company opened its doors in St. Joseph, Michigan, a maritime community on the state's southwestern shore of Lake Michigan, Thomas had practiced his craft for nearly half a century.

A FRESH START

In the autumn of 1870, Truscott immigrated to the United States with his wife and five children. Arriving in New York Harbor aboard the passenger ship *Virginia* on October 4, the Truscotts then traveled by rail to Chicago, where Thomas found work building small boats. Efforts to build his own business in Chicago were thwarted by Chicago's notorious political machine. Frustrated, he moved

Thomas Truscott lived the American dream. Growing up in Cornwall, England, he immigrated to the United States in 1870 and eventually created one of the most prolific and successful boatbuilding companies of his era.

HERITAGE MUSEUM AND CULTURAL CENTER, ST. JOSEPH, MICHIGAN

his family to Grand Haven, Michigan, in 1873, a shoreline community where he continued to build small craft for clients. Three years later, the Truscotts moved again, this time to Grand Rapids, located on the Grand River but inland from Lake Michigan. Here Thomas opened the doors to Truscott Boat Manufacturing Company.

Although the company had prospered during its Grand Rapids years, Thomas sought a more promising site. In the spring of 1892, sixteen years after its formation, he moved the company to St. Joseph, a lakeside town about eighty miles southwest of Grand Rapids. Then in his mid-sixties, it's conceivable that Thomas viewed this as a final opportunity to create the boatbuilding operation of his dreams. Whatever his rationale, this move led to a surge in the company's fortunes that would carry well into the twentieth century. During this same period, in other parts of the country, wood-and-canvas canoes and other small boats were being produced in quantity. However, no other midwestern company

In its heyday, Truscott Boat Manufacturing Company turned out about six hundred boats per year. They also manufactured most major components and accessories, from hardware to canvas awnings, in-house. HERITAGE MUSEUM AND CULTURAL CENTER, ST. JOSEPH, MICHIGAN

compared to Truscott in terms of the breadth and depth of its production capabilities.

In spite of the depression, the Gay Nineties were in full swing. Historian Frederick Jackson Turner had declared the American frontier closed. Bicycles were all the rage, and the first of the newfangled automobiles—horseless carriages, some called them—were raising dust and frightening horses as they sputtered and backfired along the country's mostly dirt roads. Radio waves were beginning to crackle through the atmosphere, and electric lights were flickering on to illuminate the continent. Best of all, Americans were enjoying more leisure time.

By the 1890s, industry was flourishing in the town of St. Joseph. Wells-Higman produced wooden boxes and baskets for southwest Michigan's abundant fruit-growing region, while St. Joseph Iron Works manufactured basket-making machines. Morrison Tub and Pail Factory was one of the nation's largest wooden-ware manufacturers in the 1880s. Truscott was a natural fit for this maritime community, whose heritage dated back to the early nineteenth century as a freight-forwarding station. Trade goods from the East that were shipped through the Erie Canal and from Great Lakes ports arrived in St. Joseph by schooner where they were loaded aboard keelboats bound for upriver towns and villages. Locally grown commodities such as wheat, flour, fruit, and other agricultural products were shipped in the opposite direction. Great Lakes traffic and teeming harbor activity created a demand for boats as far back as 1832, when commercial vessels ranging from launches to schooners were built at St. Joseph.

The southwestern Michigan location proved to be ideal for Truscott's needs. Lumber, mainly white oak, was abundant. Railroad lines connected with the rest of the nation, allowing the company to bring in raw materials and to ship finished boats to customers. In addition, commercial shipping offered an alternate means of transportation. The channel into the St. Joseph River and to the harbor, which had been developed years before by the US government, provided access to Lake Michigan, where sea trials of the company's larger boats could be conducted.

Truscott's first St. Joseph shop was on the second floor of a building that was a stone's throw from the harbor. From that shop, it was a leisurely stroll down the bluffs to the shore where sugar-sand beaches and dunes sprawled north and south as far as the eye could see. Immediately across the river, on the north bank, sat the town of Benton Harbor. These small communities, known locally as the "Twin Cities," would enjoy the fruits of Thomas Truscott's enterprise for years to come.

Truscott had a clear and ambitious vision. His boats and all of their major components were to be made within the company's facility: hulls, oars,

Truscott launches ranged from 16' to more than 50' LOA and were available with a variety of options. This 53' launch was one of the larger, better-outfitted models.

HERITAGE MUSEUM AND CULTURAL CENTER, ST. JOSEPH, MICHIGAN

SAME general style and finish as the $30.00 outfit, only that this boat is fifteen feet long, forty-two inches beam; has two sets row locks and ash oars; specially adapted for boat livery service (as boat has a wide and long bottom which makes it steady) on any water, the good shear making it a thorough sea boat. Are built like the higher priced boats, with oak keel running full length instead of the wide bottom board of soft wood, as built by others when selling low priced boats. *The best value ever offered to boating people. Strictly first-class.*

A FIFTEEN foot boat like cut shown, being pointed at both ends; is a fine sea boat, steady and a very light rower; well painted inside and out, with seats, gunwales, oars, etc.; finished on the natural wood with varnish; a complete set of canvas cushions, rudder and yoke, the Truscott anchor, two sets Truscott patent foot braces and combination row locks, and two pair spruce straight blade oars, anchor and painter lines. Name painted on both sides of the boat if desired. There is not a boat built anywhere in the world that has as many good points for its price.

FOURTEEN feet long, forty-one inches beam, fourteen and one-half inches deep; three seats with brown canvas covered cushions stuffed with cork; rudder with steering lines; Truscott patent adjustable foot braces and combination rowlocks with two pairs of copper-tipped, varnished spruce oars; anchor with line; painted three coats paint up to lower edge of shear strake and inside under the ribs (notice how close they are); the shear strake, wales, seats and ribs finished on the natural wood with spar varnish; name painted in a tasty manner—no extra cost.

THE boat is large, roomy, good depth and back support for stern seat; has set of well made and durable corduroy cushions, rudder, yoke and steering lines; the Truscott anchor, painter for tying to docks; two sets Truscott patent adjustable foot braces and combination rowlocks, and two pair spruce spoon oars, making a complete outfit not surpassed for the purpose. This boat is well and durably finished throughout with three coats spar varnish on the natural wood, and is copper fastened; ribs but three inches apart, making a fine appearing, strong and serviceable boat, and is perfectly safe in any water for children to use, and rows so easy that the smallest of them can row the boat. Name painted on boat in neat and tasty style at no extra cost. Boat is fifteen feet long, forty-two inches beam, fourteen and one-half inches deep, square stern.

WITH this we show a larger size and a more highly trimmed boat than our sixty-five dollar outfit. Sixteen feet long, forty two inches beam, fifteen inches deep amidship, has four seats, full set of best quality corduroy cushions, canvas bottom for floor, two pair spruce spoon oars, rudder, anchor and lines. All metal work is made of polished brass and nickel plated. Well finished on the natural wood with four coats of spar varnish; name painted on both bows at no extra cost. Planking is of cedar or cypress, trimmings are of cherry or walnut, ribs but three inches apart and copper riveted on washers to planking. We are sure this will please you, as the difference in price is more than put in in the extra finish, as it is indeed handsome.

THIS boat is now built two feet longer and has many new and desirable features added, making it a boat, in our opinion, as fine as anyone could wish for, as it surely combines every desirable feature for comfort and ease that could possibly be attached to a row boat. Is seventeen feet long, forty-two inches beam, sixteen inches deep; copper riveted, planking of cedar or cypress, cherry carvings and trimmings. All seats caned (as shown where cushion is left off); also back rest, which is reversible, so that passengers in after seats may face each other, if desired; silk plush cushions for all seats. Awning so made that it may be put up and taken down in a few moments. Boat is fitted with Truscott patent adjustable foot braces and combination rowlocks and two pair spruce spoon oars copper tipped and varnished, rudder and lines. All metal work is nickel plated on polished brass. Boat finished throughout with four coats spar varnish and rubbed to a high gloss. The general elegance of the carvings, style and finish, will have to be seen to be appreciated. Name painted in gold leaf and shaded.

SHOWING two views of one of the boats which we furnished to the African agents of the Schlitz Brewing Co., and which we shipped to Cape Town, South Africa.

Truscott offered a variety of small boats and accessories for rowing and sailing. HERITAGE MUSEUM AND CULTURAL CENTER, ST. JOSEPH, MICHIGAN

engines, brass fittings, hand-stitched seat cushions, canvas awnings, anchors, lanterns, and propellers. Truscott went ahead and expanded the company's product line to include much larger boats, in spite of the current state of the economy.

As 1893 dawned, the country was reeling from natural calamities that had exacerbated the already dire financial concerns. Drought-ravaged farmers—particularly in the Midwest—were short on cash to pay debts, driving down the value of their land. The Philadelphia & Reading Railroad, a major Eastern line, collapsed in the final days of President Benjamin Harrison's administration. Hundreds of bank and business failures soon followed. The stock market plunged as European investors pulled their funds.

On the Great Lakes, steamers were laid up without contracts as economic news worsened. Discussions among the Truscotts must have raised serious questions: Would the market for recreational boats collapse? Would raw materials be readily available? How reliable were the surviving railroads and commercial shipping firms? Were the company's banks strong enough to survive the downturn? An ironic twist of fate provided answers from an unlikely place, with the stars seemingly aligned for the Truscotts.

MANNA FROM CHICAGO

The World's Columbian Exposition, also known as the Chicago World's Fair, took place in 1893. It celebrated the four hundredth anniversary of Christopher Columbus's landing in America (delayed by one year). Although the city that had driven the family to Michigan two decades earlier, Chicago now awarded Truscott its first significant contract: supplying scores of watercraft for the Exposition: gondolas, rowing boats, and steam launches.

The Columbian Exposition featured nearly two hundred new buildings of classical architecture, along with picturesque canals and lagoons, all of which spread across 630 acres along Chicago's waterfront. Displays offered a romantic look into America's future, including the recreational boats produced by Truscott. In addition to supplying boats that moved the fair's twenty-seven million

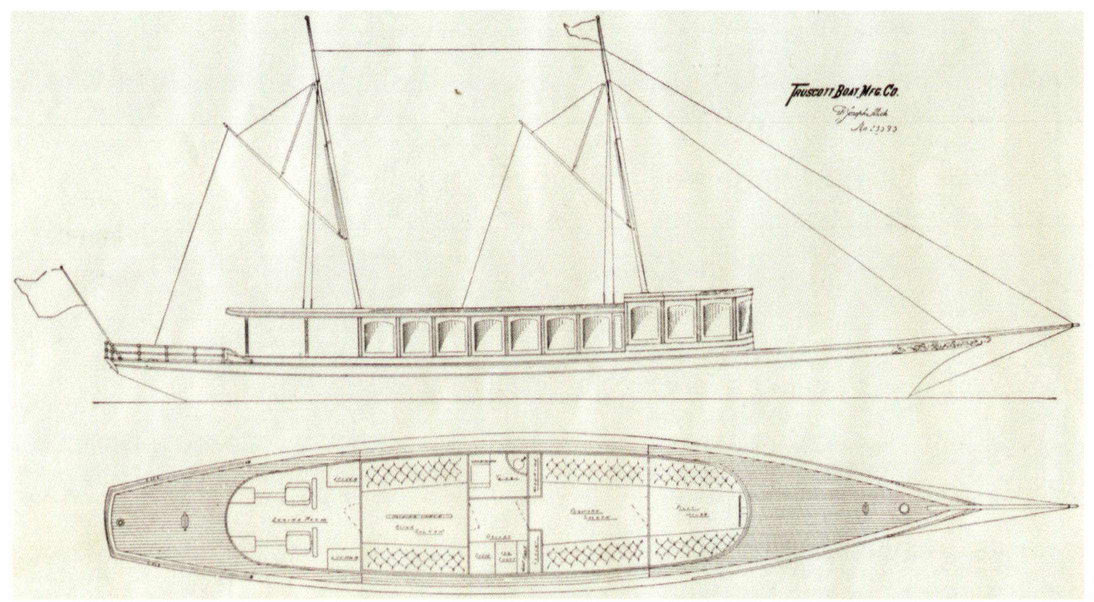

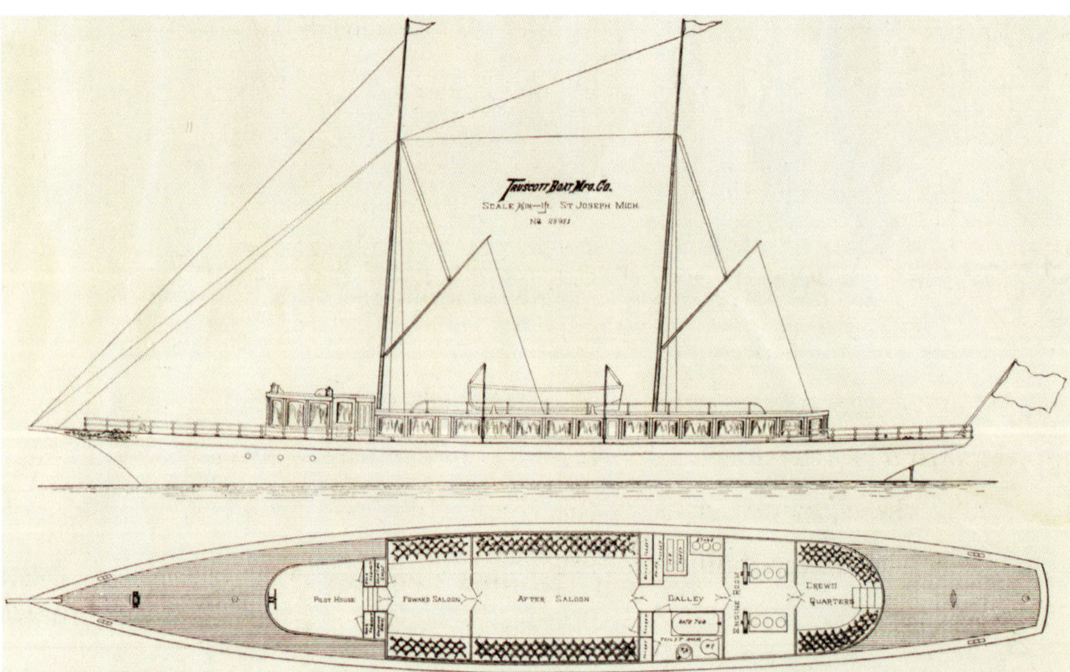

The outboard profile and deck plan for a 60' cruiser (top) gives a sense of the high style that a Truscott yacht could provide. The 85' cruiser (bottom), like her smaller sister, displays the fanciful fantail stern, another telltale sign of elegance and fine craftsmanship. Both of these yachts were offered in the early 1900s. HERITAGE MUSEUM AND CULTURAL CENTER, ST. JOSEPH, MICHIGAN

visitors—equal to approximately half of the US population at the time—between these wondrous sights, Truscott exhibited its stylish rowing boats, for which it received an award of excellence for design and craftsmanship.

The Columbian Exposition jump-started Truscott and prepared it for the next half-century. If the Panic of 1893 had dealt a blow to America's psyche, you couldn't prove it by looking at Thomas Truscott and his workers. Appearing undaunted, they rolled up their sleeves with a view toward expansion. The company acquired the former Morrison Tub and Pail Factory on the Morrison Channel, an offshoot of the river. This prime site further accommodated Truscott's progressive "under-one-roof" vision and provided additional space to expand the company's boat line. The company's reputation, bolstered by the Chicago World's Fair, led to an increase in orders from North American and overseas clients. By 1897, the economic crisis was abating, and recreational boating was gaining popularity as predicted. But the other shoe was about to drop.

Around the turn of the twentieth century, the best and, in most cases, the only mode of overland transport was by rail. Truscott made the most of this, shipping launches in custom boxcars with specially designed end doors and billboard-sized advertisements on the sides. HERITAGE MUSEUM AND CULTURAL CENTER, ST. JOSEPH, MICHIGAN

On September 10, 1899, fire swept through the boat shop and finishing room, two machine shops, the foundry, nickel plating, polishing rooms, cushion department, and business offices. Only a large warehouse and two storage buildings remained standing. The gutted factory with its crumbling brick walls lay in ruins. Such a fire could be the death knell for any company, yet ninety days later Truscott Boat Manufacturing Company was back, operating at full strength.

The 1900 Truscott catalog published only weeks after the catastrophe reflected the Truscotts' optimism. "We claim to furnish better boats and machinery than others for your money," it declared. "All of the buildings and their equipments [*sic*] are brand new (our recent fire compelled this). . . ." Indeed, the fire of 1899 could be viewed as a stroke of good fortune, allowing the Truscotts to design a new manufacturing complex to meet their specific needs. They developed new equipment such as elevated tracks to rapidly launch completed boats in the adjacent Morrison Channel, and railroad boxcars with specially designed end doors in which to load and ship 20' to 30' launches. Boats as long as 75' and as wide as 12' were shipped on railroad flatcars adapted for that purpose.

Through the early 1900s, Truscott manufactured launches in five sizes from 16' to 30' LOA.

"It will be our aim to keep these boats in stock, so quick deliveries can be made," the company explained in its catalogs. Within a few years, Henry Ford would employ a similar strategy in marketing and selling motorcars, making stock models available at a reasonable price to a broad spectrum of society. In addition, Truscott offered other boats of varying lengths and uses, and with a variety of available accessories. The larger launches and yachts over 30' in length were custom built to the owner's specifications. As a result, Truscott boats were valued for their exquisite lines and quality appointments.

By 1906 the workforce numbered seven hundred and not only attracted craftsmen from the Twin Cities region, but from other Michigan and Indiana communities as well. It had by then become the largest company in St. Joseph. Many skilled workers had followed the company to St. Joseph from Grand Rapids. Six hundred wooden boats per year came out of the Truscott shops, from simple rowboats to 85' yachts.

This 25' launch came equipped with a swing awning. HERITAGE MUSEUM AND CULTURAL CENTER, ST. JOSEPH, MICHIGAN

QUALITY CONSTRUCTION

"We have plenty of good workmen, because we operate the shops the year round, pay good wages, [our] buildings are all light, roomy, well heated and ventilated, and equipped with all modern conveniences to maintain their health and spirits," the company boasted with pride. "As a result, these men stay with us and grow more proficient." These labor policies and practices were highly progressive for the time.

Quality control was a company hallmark. Department foremen were charged with replacing defective materials or correcting poor workmanship. Piecework was eschewed because "too much of such work can be covered up." In addition, all raw materials were purchased directly from the producers, rather than from jobbing houses. Only high-quality materials were selected for Truscott boats. Frames, wearing parts, and pieces subject to strain were fashioned from nearly flawless straight-grained white oak. Planks were shaped from cypress, "unless otherwise specified, due to its superiority." Deck-beams, breast-hooks, knees, and coamings were also made from white oak. Copper fastenings were used, except when "special purposes" called for galvanized iron. The same level of skill and high-quality materials were used throughout Truscott's entire line. The only differences were in the furnishings and finishes, as requested by customers. Various accessories and finishes were available. Black cherry decks, covering boards, interior paneling, seating, and bulkhead coverings, for example, could be ordered for an additional 5 percent of any boat's base price. Honduras mahogany trim was available for another 10 percent.

NEW BOATS BY THE HUNDREDS

Although Truscott did not operate assembly lines like those adopted by Ford and the fledgling automobile industry, it produced boats by the hundreds annually. On any given day, there were more than two dozen launches (ranging from 16' to 50' in length) in various stages of completion.

At the same time, larger boats, generally custom orders, shared the space along with the dozens of craftsmen who worked on them. Industrial machinery—planers, bandsaws, table saws, and sanders—facilitated the work where possible. The 1901 Truscott catalog explained, "everything that can be done by machinery is done [by machine]. However, it is a fact that the bulk of the work on boats is of necessity hand work."

Because the growing number of launches seemed to be eclipsing orders for smaller boats, Truscott

This 32' Mackinaw sailboat was built in the early 1900s for the US Life Saving Service for use on Lake Superior. Mackinaw boats were versatile craft used for fishing and recreation on the Great Lakes. HERITAGE MUSEUM AND CULTURAL CENTER, ST. JOSEPH, MICHIGAN

operated a separate shop for building its rowboats, leaving the larger shop for the launches. "No, we don't build as many [rowing boats] as we did a few years ago, but we still manage to get a few orders," the company literature explained. Despite the reduction in this business segment, the rowboat shop staff exceeded a dozen workers.

Launches ranging from 16' to 30'—the company's bread-and-butter products through the early 1900s—were carried in stock. Construction details were published in the company's annual catalogs. Frames were steam-bent to shape and spaced 5" to 9" on center, depending on a boat's size and thickness of planking. Stretchers (crosspieces for rowers to brace their feet) were "secured by floors closely fitted to the keel." Wide planking stock was available, allowing planks to be shaped and fitted in long lengths. Butts were reinforced between the frames. Beefy inwales were bolted through frame heads and the sheerstrake. Deck beams, breast hooks, knees, and coaming pieces were sawn to shape. Narrow strakes of decking laid parallel to the keel were fastened to the sheerstrake and

inwales. Finally, joints were caulked and payed with colored putty to better match the finish.

Bulkheads were installed across the forward and aft ends of the cockpit, with the forward bulkhead being watertight. Seats were built along both sides of the cockpit forward of the motor. Space underneath the seats—accessed through "lids of good size . . . fitted with brass hinges and lifts"—accommodated storage. On either side of the motor, raised lockers were built, with one housing the battery and the other tools. The center section of the floorboards was removable, allowing access to the bilge. Coamings were made from solid white oak. They were steam-bent and then reinforced with "coaming knees." The lockers, deck, and floor were well ventilated to extend the life of the wood and keep the boat fresh for the enjoyment of the crew.

Once final touches were completed in the construction shops, the boats were shifted to the finishing room, where between thirty and forty workers applied paint and varnish. Up to thirty boats could be found there at almost any time. Each remained for at least fifteen days to ensure a durable finish was achieved. "Good varnish and paint dries slowly, so order your boat early," the company advised prospective buyers. Unless otherwise requested, a boat's topsides received three coats of paint up to the sheerstrake. Three coats of spar varnish were applied to the sheerstrake, decks, coamings, and all cockpit surfaces. Inside storage areas received three coats of paint to protect and preserve the wood. Finally, the bottom of the boat below the waterline was coated with either green or red copper-based antifouling paint.

Launches came with their motors installed and ready to run, together with an array of standard accessories: a United States ensign, a burgee with the name of the boat sewn in (or one of a special design), polished staffs and sockets, a pair of oarlocks and oars, an anchor and lines, mooring lines, a steering wheel placed forward of or alongside the motor (both locations on boats 22½' LOA and larger), and cleats, chocks, and deck steering gear. One set of seat cushions filled with cork shavings and faced with hair—which could serve as life preservers—were also standard. Boat names were applied on both sides of the bow in "neatly shaded" gold leaf or in cast brass letters. For an additional cost, launch customers seeking a custom look could order trim in oak, cherry, or mahogany. They could also order, in a variety of colors, striped awnings supported by substantial, polished stanchions, as well as deck rails.

Sintz gasoline engines had been used in early production, but in order to fulfill his vision of manufacturing every component, Truscott developed a line of gasoline-powered marine engines called Truscott Vapor Marine Motors. In 1901, 10-, 12-, and 14-hp models came as standard equipment in Truscott launches. The only other exception to the company's "under-one-roof" philosophy was a line of marine steam engines manufactured by Upton, which were offered as an alternative to Truscott's standard gasoline engines. These engines, as well as a line of marine boilers necessary for their function, conformed to US marine laws of the time.

TRUSCOTT AND THE WORLD

Truscott, by the turn of the twentieth century, had established sales offices in New York, Boston, Philadelphia, Buffalo, Chicago, Detroit, St. Paul,

New Orleans, Mobile, and Washington, DC. With clients all across America and a growing presence in foreign countries, the company developed a network to transport its boats by rail and ship to customers worldwide. At the company's height, international sales offices operated in places like London, Amsterdam, Antwerp, Victoria (British Columbia), and Constantinople. Truscott boats were found even in the farthest reaches of Africa and the Pacific. In addition to recreational boats, Truscott built working craft for the US Life Saving Service, the US Lighthouse Service, and the Brazilian navy, as well as boats for commercial fishing and polar exploration. Always on the forefront of innovation, Truscott published a quarterly newsletter called *The Launch,* which featured the latest offerings and included letters and photos from satisfied Truscott customers worldwide.

Thomas Truscott died on February 15, 1905, after a brief bout with pneumonia in Pass Christian, Mississippi, knowing that his dream had been realized and would carry forward under the guidance of his sons.

About a decade later, during World War I, Truscott workmen went to other boat shops in St. Joseph and Benton Harbor to produce boats for the US Navy. Once the war ended in 1918, the company resumed normal operations. The Great Depression, which began with the Wall Street crash of 1929, sent the pleasure-craft market—particularly the market for expensive private yachts—into a downward spiral. Truscott never really recovered. John Truscott died in 1938, followed by Edward Truscott in 1939. James Truscott continued to manage the business until 1940 when he sold out to a Chicago firm that retained the Truscott name.

Thomas Truscott's dream—as brilliant as a shooting star—all but vanished but left in its wake a legacy that lives on in the archives and collections of the Heritage Museum and Cultural Center in St. Joseph. Though it has now become a modest lakeside place, some people here can still remember when their fair city once held a titan of industry in its hands and take pride that there was such a time.

TRUSCOTT ROWBOAT—A TREASURE WAS FOUND

Around 1897, New Hampshire railroad magnate Walter Aiken purchased a 17', Whitehall-style wooden rowboat, built by Truscott Boat Manufacturing Company in St. Joseph, Michigan, for his summer island home. The cost was $125. The little rowboat was planked in cypress and trimmed in black cherry. She was meticulously outfitted with copper-tipped spoon-bladed oars, bronze oarlocks, a stretcher (foot brace) for rowing, a cane seat and backrest for the passenger facing forward or aft, and three gold velour cushions filled with shredded cork.

The boat remained in Aiken's family for seventy years, preserved in a covered boathouse. In February 2004, over a century after the boat was built, Kenneth Pott, then executive director of the Heritage Museum and Cultural Center in St. Joseph, Michigan, received an anonymous email offering to sell the artifact to the museum. The message expressed a wish to return her to her rightful home on the southeastern shore of Lake Michigan. The asking price was $12,000, well under its appraised value of $25,000.

Pott was excited and concerned at the same time. If the emailer's offer was legitimate, the boat would also greatly interest better-known maritime museums across America. After responding to the initial message, Pott learned that the mysterious query had come from a man in Brattleboro, Vermont, who had purchased the boat from the Aiken family thirty years earlier. The man, Jon Knickerbocker, believed that the boat should be in a museum rather than in private hands. As Pott had surmised, larger maritime museums had shown interest—but fortunately for Heritage, Knickerbocker was most interested in returning the boat to St. Joseph.

Few Truscott boats remain in existence. This one—in pristine condition—found her way home to St. Joseph, Michigan, in 2004. She matches the description of the $125 model (called *Ideal*) in the Truscott catalog spread on page 120. GEORGE D. JEPSON

By early 1942, America was gearing up for war, and the Truscott Boat Manufacturing Company was under new ownership. Wartime pulled the company's attention to build crash boats (near the top) and other boats for military service. HERITAGE MUSEUM AND CULTURAL CENTER, ST. JOSEPH, MICHIGAN

Within a month of the first contact, Knickerbocker asked Heritage to make a commitment. Realizing that the chance to obtain a Truscott boat like this would likely never come again, Pott pressed on in his search for funding. After many hair-raising moments, a former Heritage board member offered $6,000 as a matching challenge grant to raise the necessary funds. Knickerbocker agreed to this approach. A fundraising campaign successfully brought in the remaining money.

On May 18, 2004—after 107 years—the icon representing St. Joseph and Michigan maritime history returned to the city where she was built. The sleek little rowboat, with her elegant appointments, is now displayed in the Heritage Museum and Cultural Center, whose archives include examples of Truscott's promotional catalogs, historical photographs, drawings of some of their designs, testimonial statements from owners, and many other records.

"Roaring Dan" Seavey

GREAT LAKES ROGUE

By the time Captain Dan Seavey ("Roaring Dan") was apprehended in 1908 for piracy by the US Revenue Cutter Service on Lake Michigan, he was already infamous. Nevertheless, the Seavey saga, enriched by vivid—and sometimes fictitious—contemporary newspaper accounts, still resonates a century later among those interested in the lore of the Great Lakes.

Daniel W. Seavey, born in Maine on March 23, 1865, was the son of a schooner captain. As a boy, he longed to go to sea. So, by his own account, at age thirteen, he left home to sail aboard "downeast" schooners. At eighteen, he enlisted in the US Navy, serving for over two years. During the late 1880s, Seavey arrived in the Great Lakes region, settling near Marinette, Wisconsin, where he married and had two daughters. The family later moved to Milwaukee, where Seavey farmed, operated a fishing business, and ran two saloons.

Seavey was an imposing man physically, with a prizefighter's build. Standing 6'4" or more and weighing 250 pounds, with a barrel chest, he was a well-known bar-room brawler, using his reach and heavy fists to advantage against local challengers. On occasion, he fought for money.

During the winter of 1904, Seavey squared off in Frankfort, Michigan, with Mitch Love, a downstate bruiser, inside a shoveled circle on the harbor's frozen surface. The bareknuckle match carried on for almost two hours, with Seavey eventually battering Love bloody and netting Roaring Dan the

Dan Seavey, known to some as "Roaring Dan," became a legend in his own time on the Great Lakes. **PUBLIC DOMAIN**

main purse and winnings from several side bets placed by his supporters.

In 1898, lured by news of the Klondike Gold Rush, Seavey abruptly sold his farm and two saloons, abandoned his family, invested $10,000 in a mining venture, and headed north to Alaska, hoping to find his fortune, along with one hundred thousand other prospectors. Two years later, as a new century dawned, he was flat broke and returned to Milwaukee to become a bartender.

"The only time I made any real money in Alaska was when I got $500 for hoisting up a large safe that had fallen through the floor of a saloon," he told the *Escanaba Daily Press* in 1930. "There was a lot of money in the safe, and the owners had been trying for a couple of weeks to raise her up to the main floor."

Although impoverished, Seavey moved to Escanaba, on Little Bay de Noc on northern Lake Michigan, and acquired a swift 42' two-masted schooner which he named *Wanderer*. The means to finance the purchase remain a mystery, but this marked the onset of his notorious, often shady, exploits. *Wanderer*'s crew was a gang of thugs that soon became notorious. They'd slip silently into harbors after dark without running lights, steal from other ships, wharves, and waterfront warehouses, and then vanish before dawn. To be fair, *Wanderer* also transported legitimate freight, including fresh fruit and timber products; but thievery and venison poaching proved more lucrative.

Dan Seavey's purchase of the schooner *Wanderer* marked the onset of his notorious, often shady, exploits. PUBLIC DOMAIN

On occasion, Seavey even operated the schooner as a profitable bordello on Lake Michigan, dropping anchor offshore in communities like Escanaba, Fayette, Garden, and Nahma, where working men looked forward to *Wanderer*'s arrival on weekends and paydays, with prostitutes and liquor aboard. As a result, brothels flourished in Great Lakes ports. Although local authorities attempted to halt the disreputable practice, activities in harbors beyond the waterline were beyond their jurisdiction.

Roaring Dan's most celebrated action, pirating the 52' schooner *Nellie Johnson*, secured his legacy in Great Lakes maritime history, which newspapers tended to embellish (see sidebar on page 136). On June 11, 1908, with the *Johnson* moored in Grand Haven, Michigan, Seavey went aboard and plied three watchmen with liquor. After his crew had carried the intoxicated sailors ashore, the schooner set sail for Chicago, laden with valuable cedar posts. Failing to unload the cargo and perhaps sensing the law in his wake, Seavey crossed the lake to Frankfort, left the *Johnson*, and returned aboard his schooner *Wanderer*. Observing this, the armed 178' federal revenue cutter *Tuscarora* headed off in pursuit. A lively chase ensued, but finally, *Wanderer* hove-to; Seavey was arrested, clapped in irons, and charged with piracy—a hanging offense in those days, but the charges were reduced and later dropped when *Nellie Johnson*'s owner failed to appear in court.

Over the years, Seavey operated legitimate businesses out of Escanaba that were totally at odds with his previous immoral life. "Dan Seavey, skipper of the *Mary Alice*, is building a dock at Squaw Point, where his boat is taking berry pickers daily," the *Escanaba Morning Press* reported on July 29, 1920. "Mr. Seavey also reports that berries are plentiful in the Squaw Point region and that the *Mary Alice* has been handling a very satisfactory amount of passenger business." About the same time, he had a half interest in a resort, which he sold in 1924.

Seavey's story ended with an ironic twist. Near the end of his career, he changed sides and served with the US Marshals Service, working against poachers and smugglers. He retired in 1927, and resided in a local boardinghouse in Escanaba. In the late 1930s, he moved to a farm near Peshtigo, Wisconsin, where he lived with his daughter until he died on February 14, 1949.

DAN SEAVEY

"Pirate on Lake Stopped by Shot"
The Inter Ocean, Chicago,
Illinois, June 30, 1908

Thirteen men on a dead man's chest,
Yo, ho, ho, and a bottle of rum;
Drink and the devil had done for the rest,
Yo, Ho, Ho, and a bottle of rum.

—Stevenson

Skipper Dan Seavey stood with his hand on the wheel of the two-masted schooner *Wanderer*. In a voice that had the deep boom of a fog horn he shouted to the crew: "Move, you son of a sea cook, you waterlogged landlubber. Get hold of the top-gallant sheet and pull in those peak halyards."

In less than a jiffy, every stitch of canvas on the *Wanderer* was thrown to the breeze and the craft stood off to the northwest, scudding before a twenty knot wind like a huge white winged bird. Masts bent and creaked and the boat trembled from bowsprit to stern, but held her course, spray dashing from her prow in huge clouds.

Skipper Seavey picked up his glasses and glanced anxiously windward. Lying close down on the horizon, her white hull scarcely descernible [*sic*], marked only by the stream of black smoke pouring from her funnels, was the government revenue cutter *Tuscarora*, Captain U. H. Uberroth commanding. The smoke from the *Tuscarora* double in volume, she took a course dead astern of the *Wanderer*, and then began the prettiest pursuit the great lakes [*sic*] have seen for years.

He reckons poorly who declares the days of the black flag, the days of the swashbuckler of the seas swashing on his buckler, ended with the death of Captain Kidd.

On board the *Wanderer* was Skipper Seavey, charged with piracy. On the revenue cutter was United States Marshal Thomas H. Currier, armed with a warrant for his arrest.

Sailing as she never sailed before, fairly lifting her long, slender hull through the crested waves, the *Wanderer* sped onward, Michigan shore line fading into the distance, the broad expanse of the lake ahead.

The race began late Saturday afternoon, when the revenue cutter sighted the schooner ten miles off shore from Frankfort, Mich.

Back in the *Tuscarora* engineers were crowding every ounce of steam into the cylinders. From the bodies of stokers and coal passers perspiration ran

The US revenue cutter *Tuscarora* pursued Dan Seavey attempting to escape aboard his schooner *Wanderer*. PUBLIC DOMAIN

WILD CHASE ON LAKE; CUTTER FIRES AT SHIP

Piracy Stories Are Recalled by the Experience of Dan Seavey, Placed Under Arrest.

USURPED VESSEL IS CHARGE

Romantic Nautical Adventure Results from the Alleged Seizure of a Lumber Schooner.

like water. The boat quivered from prow to stern with the throbbing engines and plowed through the seas, waves dashing as high as the bridge.

As if fright lent speed to her keel, the schooner fairly flew before the wind; the revenue cutter, with a heavy draft, churned through the seas behind her. But the contest was unequal. Four triple expansion engines on the revenue cutter ate up the lead held by the sailer. Closer and closer drew the government boat.

On the deck of the sailing craft a frenzied crew drew taut this rope and that, bending every effort to gain an inch more speed.

Signal Is Disregarded

With only 500 yards between the boats the cutter flew a government signal, calling on the sailer to heave to. The signal was disregarded.

A white puff of smoke. Zing! and a twelve pound shot whizzed over the deck of the *Wanderer*.

Seavey surrendered. The boat came up into the wind and soon an armed crew from the cutter boarded and took possession. Seavey was taken on board the cutter, locked up in the brig, and then the boat headed for Chicago. The harbor was reached late Sunday afternoon.

Yesterday morning Seavey was given a preliminary hearing before United States Commissioner Foote on a charge of piracy. Following the hearing he was released on bond and he turned over to the federal authorities his own boat, the *Wanderer*, as security. Seavey will appear before the federal grand jury July 7.

Charges Dan With Piracy

Charges against Dan Seavey were filed June 17 by Captain Robert J. McCormick of the schooner *Nellie Johnson*. The specific charge was that Seavey had usurped command of the *Nellie Johnson* and had sailed the craft away from the harbor in Grand Haven, Mich., with a consignment of lumber from the Lake Superior regions.

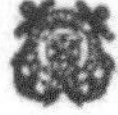

UNITED STATES REVENUE-CUTTER SERVICE.

STEAMER TUSCARORA.

Milwaukee, Wisconsin,
June 29, 1908.

The Honorable,
    The Secretary of the Treasury,
        Washington, D.C.

Sir:
    I have the honor to confirm telegram sent to the Department on arrival at Chicago on the 28th instant. TUSCARORA arrived Chicago to-day with prisoner captured on schooner Wanderer high seas, 7 miles S.W. Frankfort 3:30 P.M. 27, Nellie Johnson located Frankfort left in possession lawful owners.

Respectfully,
P. H. Uberroth,
Captain, U.S.R.C.S.,
Commanding.

Captain U. H. Uberroth notified the US secretary of the treasury by telegram following Dan Seavey's capture.

The naval laws which make piracy a crime say:

"Every person who on the high seas commits the crime of piracy, as defined by the law of nations, and is afterward brought into or found in the United States shall suffer death."

The specific crime with which Seavey was charged, however, was that of running away with a vessel on which he had been a seaman, which means that he may be, if found guilty, fined not more than $10,000 or imprisoned at hard labor for not more than ten years.

Tells How It Happened

To United States Marshal Thomas H. Currier was assigned the task of running down Dan Seavey and the stolen *Nellie Johnson*.

"I boarded the revenue cutter a week ago Saturday," said Currier yesterday. "We steamed first to Michigan City, then over to Benton Harbor, and then to every port on the Michigan shore until we reached Point Betsey. Near Point Betsey is the Frankfort harbor, and there we found the *Nellie Johnson*. She had six feet of water in her hold, but all of her cargo. Out at sea from Frankfort we sighted the *Wanderer* and gave chase. The *Wanderer* belongs to Seavey. He had sailed the *Nellie Johnson* into port and then started on another cruise in his own boat.

Dan Seavey after his preliminary hearing yesterday said that the charge of piracy could not be held against him.

"I was sailing under this McCormick," he said. "We ran into Grand Haven, and he left the boat. He was on shore I don't know how many days. He deserted her. That's what the crew thought. The boat was in bad shape, and I thought it was best to get her into harbor at Frankfort as soon as possible. So I sailed her up there and tied her up to the dock, not knowing what had become of her captain. I started out on a cruise of my own, and the next thing I knew was the revenue boat giving me chase."

Cutter Is Laid Up

The revenue cutter laid up for repairs at the conclusion of the long search for the missing *Nellie Johnson*. Describing the search and the race with the *Wanderer*, Captain Uberroth said last night:

"Upon request of District Attorney Sims and United States Commissioner Foote of Chicago, who had been informed of the seizure of the vessel Nellie Johnson, I was asked to set out on a hunt for the man. We took on board our vessel United States Marshal Thomas Currier of Chicago, who had in his possession a warrant for Seavey's arrest for piracy, and the arrest of his two companions wherever they might be found.

"The master of the schooner also came aboard with us in the hope that the cutter would fall in with his schooner, and he would recover his property. We set sail without knowing where to look for the stolen craft–none knew where she had gone."

Sails For Frankfort, Mich.

Captain Uberroth told of his fruitless search for several days after visiting many ports. He finally got the word that the stolen schooner was moored in the river at Frankfort, Mich.

"When we received the news we were told that Seavey was about to set sail for across the lake," he continued, "but the hour we could not ascertain, and we were in a quandary.

"We waited all night for the schooner to appear. We saw no signs of the vessel, however, and at daybreak we went up beyond the bluff, where we dropped anchor, to telephone the captain of the life saving crew and get him to notify us when Seavey left. We had hardly done this when we sighted the schooner under full sail with a good, stiff breeze, sailing directly out into the lake.

"As we had a good description of Seavey's schooner, the *Wanderer*, we were certain of our boat, and steamed after her. It was an exciting trip. She had a good start, but we fired up and made fast time, with the result that in an hour or two we caught up with the schooner. We hailed the man and ordered him to heave to.

Armed Crew Sent Aboard

"I then sent an armed crew, with their arms concealed, for he was known to be a desperate man, with instructions to bring him aboard. This was done, and when he reached our vessel the warrant was read by Marshal Currier, and Seavey was put under arrest. The vessel was sent back and moored to a wharf at Frankfort.

"Seavey was surprised, to say the least. He said that we never would have caught him had he had another half hour's start.

"It was one of the most exciting trips we have had, and the capture, together with the uncertainty of finding him, kept our crew busy."

Marshal Currier said last night:

"I have chased criminals all my life, but this was the most thrilling experience of many years. I never before chased a pirate with a steamship, and probably never will again. But of all the 'jolly pirates' Seavey is the jolliest."

The schooner *J. T. Wing* on Lake St. Clair, a pencil drawing by Michigan marine artist Robert McGreevy. As a young Great Lakes mariner, Henry Barkhausen sailed in the vessel in 1937. The experience deepened his passion for the maritime heritage of the Lakes. © ROBERT MCGREEVY

CHAPTER 8

Henry Barkhausen
A GREAT LAKES MARINER REMEMBERS

On a midsummer evening in 1937, the 147' three-masted schooner *J. T. Wing*—the last commercial wooden sailing ship on the Great Lakes—pointed up Green Bay under a following breeze. Climbing aloft, Henry Barkhausen reset the main topsail as the schooner jibed, spreading her wings in the waning dusk. A volunteer hand, twenty-two-year-old Barkhausen had boarded the schooner at the Northern Paper Mill Docks in Green Bay, Wisconsin, eager to taste life under working sail.

Already a seasoned freshwater sailor, Barkhausen's adventure aboard the *Wing* (ex-*Charles F. Gordon*, ex-*J. O. Webster*, and ex-*Oliver H. Perry*) deepened his passion for sailing and Great Lakes

Henry Noyes Barkhausen spent a lifetime sailing the Great Lakes and studying their rich maritime history. GEORGE D. JEPSON

The schooner *Lucia A. Simpson*, seen here loaded with stacked lumber and logs in the 1930s, was the vessel that first sparked Henry Barkhausen's maritime interest in 1926. COURTESY OF THUNDER BAY NATIONAL MARINE SANCTUARY

maritime history, a course he would pursue for decades. Learning about the shoal-draft, centerboard schooners indigenous to the sweetwater seas became a lifelong quest. The result was a priceless collection of period photographs, rare books, builders' models, and interviews with old sailors who had shipped out in these vessels in the nineteenth century. Along the way, Barkhausen managed to establish a successful business career, wrote articles and books, and, in his spare time, built wooden boats.

On a brilliant, crisp October morning in 2014, I visited the pretty cottage Barkhausen shared with Alice, his wife of more than seven decades, in Lake Forest, Illinois. A few weeks later, he would celebrate his one hundredth birthday. Autumn leaves swirled outside his study windows under a cerulean sky. Inside, surrounded by marine paintings, nautical prints, photographs of the family's wooden boats, a builder's half model, and shelves of nautical books, I listened as Barkhausen chronicled a lifetime immersed in Great Lakes maritime culture.

President Woodrow Wilson was in the White House, and The Great War in Europe was in its early days when Barkhausen was born on December 14, 1914, in Green Bay. Around 1920, his father, Henry G. Barkhausen, acquired an old wooden schooner, sparking the boy's interest in boats. His mother, a former librarian, advanced his curiosity by introducing him to books about the sea, including one of his favorites, *Two Years Before the Mast*, by Richard Henry Dana.

In 1918, Henry's father, along with his uncle Louis H. Barkhausen, founded Northwest Engineering Works in Green Bay. The firm built 100' wooden harbor tugs and 150' steel oceangoing tugs for the US Emergency Fleet Corporation during World War I. The first harbor tug they launched was *Toiler*, a name that would surface later in the younger Barkhausen's life.

Being brought up in a maritime community, Barkhausen witnessed the last vestiges of a bygone era. On a summer's day in 1926, he observed the *Lucia A. Simpson*, a 127' three-masted topsail schooner, underway in the bay. "I hadn't realized that there were [still] commercial sailing vessels on the lakes," he said. "From then on, I fantasized about sailing in one of them; commercial sail was an early obsession."

Barkhausen attended boarding school in Connecticut during his teens in the late 1920s and early 1930s. In the summer of 1928 his father acquired a 30' Charles Mower–designed centerboard yawl built by Kidney Boat Works in DePere, Wisconsin. The boat was called *Esperanza II*, after a large, gaff-topsail ketch his father once owned. Over the next four summers, Barkhausen honed his seamanship skills on Green Bay and cruised with friends to the North Channel in Lake Huron. Barkhausen frequented the Sturgeon Bay docks, peppering fishermen with questions about Great Lakes maritime lore. He was especially interested in Mackinaw boats native to the Upper Great Lakes (Huron, Michigan, and Superior). This rugged working craft would figure—under oars and sail—in his life for years to come.

The Barkhausens sold *Esperanza II* in the early years of the Great Depression, but young Henry began longing for another sailboat during his freshman year at Yale in 1932. "A broker referred me to a boat in New Haven that was for sale for $500. It was the *Great Republic*; the sloop Howard Blackburn had sailed across the Atlantic. When I told Dad, he got scared and said, 'I guess we ought to buy a decent boat, not an old dog that probably wouldn't make it back to Sturgeon Bay.'" Father and son searched the East Coast for a suitable replacement for *Esperanza II* and, through the Sparkman & Stephens brokerage, found a 38' Alden cutter called *Mandalay*. "Dad wanted something that we might race, but this was just an ideal cruising boat, and we bought it." The next summer, with two college pals, he delivered the boat back to Sturgeon Bay, cruising up the Hudson River to Albany, transiting the Erie Canal, and sailing the final legs through Lakes Erie, Huron, and Michigan. Barkhausen sailed *Mandalay* for four seasons, making passages to the North Channel and Georgian Bay on Lake Huron, as well as the North Shore of Lake Superior, "which was really wilderness. You didn't see another yacht up there the whole month, [just] a couple of trappers and lighthouse keepers."

After graduating from Yale in the spring of 1936, he moved to Chicago to work in sales for a die-casting firm. Later that year, his father died suddenly, and *Mandalay* was put on the market. "She had been owned previously by the marine artist Frank Vining Smith," Barkhausen said. "When we offered it for sale in 1937, he bought it back."

A MACKINAW DREAM

While working in Chicago that spring, Barkhausen daydreamed of another new boat. "I wanted something cheap and started thinking about Mackinaw boats, which I had seen up in the North Channel—the 'Indian Macs.' They seemed like such able little boats. I corresponded with Grant Turner, who ran the store up in Little Current, and asked him [whether there] were any used Mackinaw boats [for sale]. He said he didn't know of any."

The schooner *J .T. Wing* sailed into Green Bay that June, laden with pulpwood. As soon as she docked, Barkhausen's phone rang in Chicago. It was a friend calling to say that passage was available on the *Wing*; she was going to Spanish River, Ontario, for another load of pulpwood.

The *J. T. Wing* in a floating drydock at Sturgeon Bay, Wisconsin, on August 22, 1937, the year Henry Barkhausen sailed aboard for Collingwood, Ontario. CARUS COLLECTION, WISCONSIN MARITIME MUSEUM

The chance to sail in a traditional commercial schooner handled by a small crew was irresistible. So, Barkhausen signed on as a volunteer crewman. "I [gained] firsthand experience handling topsails aloft, shifting the tack and sheet on the forward mast every time we came about," recalled Barkhausen, with a faraway look. "We got caught in a storm [in Georgian Bay]. That was the year the Mackinac Race had such a difficult time with a really stiff northwester. We were wind-bound near John Island, anchored in the lee. It was exciting when we finally got the anchors up. We had a northwest wind and sailed the *Wing* through the Whalesback Channel at Spanish River, which is quite a narrow passage."

Wing's master was Captain George A. Fisher, an old-time Great Lakes schoonerman. Barkhausen asked him where a Mackinaw boat might be found. Fisher mentioned a Georgian Bay fisherman who, in turn, referred him to W. Watts & Sons, who were well-respected boatbuilders in Collingwood, Ontario. Barkhausen queried Watts in May 1938 and received an immediate reply. Watts could construct a 31' square-sterned Mackinaw (also called a Huron boat) or a 33' double-ender from their original builder's models. Henry ordered the square-sterned model ($750, complete with sails), but specified that it must have topmasts, a rig he had seen on Mackinaws in a photograph (the topsails were used for racing, not fishing). The boat was finished in less than six weeks, and Barkhausen and two friends traveled by rail to Collingwood via Toronto and sailed her back to Harbor Springs, Michigan.

When Barkhausen arrived in Collingwood, her name, *Butcher Boy*, had already been painted on the transom. She was equipped with oars, two and a half tons of rock ballast under the floorboards, and eight bags of gravel to trim her. "All fishermen sailing Mackinaws used ballast," he

The fishing fleet of Collingwood, Ontario, comprising numerous Mackinaw boats, gets underway circa 1870. W. Watts & Sons were well respected Collingwood builders of Mackinaw boats, and Henry Barkhausen went to them in 1938 for a Mackinaw boat of his own. CARUS COLLECTION, WISCONSIN MARITIME MUSEUM

said. "I could see that sailing with the ballast was really critical."

The passage to Harbor Springs took five days and four nights and proved to be another learning experience. "We didn't have a motor and almost swamped it the next day in a northeaster," says Barkhausen. "You can't drive them to windward, which fishermen have confirmed."

Sailing an open Mackinaw boat offshore on the Great Lakes was no mean feat—then or now. On the second night out, Barkhausen stopped at Cabots Head on Georgian Bay. After that, Henry sailed *Butcher Boy* through each night, crossing northern Lake Huron, passing through the Mackinac Straits and into Lake Michigan. The intrepid sailors were relieved when Harbor Point and the Barkhausen summer home hove into view. On Labor Day, Barkhausen sailed the boat across Lake Michigan to Sturgeon Bay. That fall, Barkhausen enlisted "a fellow from the Palmer & Johnson yard to help and we took her lines off, because I knew she was the last of her kind, a really historic boat. We also put an engine in her the first year, after we got to Sturgeon Bay."

Alice and Henry Barkhausen aboard their Huron boat *Good News* off Harbor Springs, Michigan. COURTESY OF HENRY N. BARKHAUSEN

OLD-TIMERS' YARNS

Listening to stories shared by old-timers along the Sturgeon Bay waterfront stirred a desire within Barkhausen to learn more about the Great Lakes ships and the men who had sailed them over the previous century. He was intrigued by calendars featuring old Great Lakes sailing ships, which hung in boathouses, fishing shacks, and restaurants along the waterfront. Captain Edward Carus (see sidebar, page 156), a retired shipmaster living in Manitowoc whose career on the Great Lakes dated back to 1874, had amassed a photograph collection depicting sailing ships, steamers, and maritime scenes dating back to the 1800s. In 1937, Barkhausen visited Captain Carus to see his collection; as it turned out, Carus was looking to sell, so Barkhausen acquired it. Over the next four decades, Barkhausen added many significant items to his collection and, in 1981, sought a proper repository for the priceless treasures. He ultimately donated the Carus Collection, along with articles he had added, to the Wisconsin Maritime Museum in Manitowoc. He also donated other photographs, books, and documents to Bowling Green State University in Ohio.

Captain Dan Seavey (see Chapter 7), a notorious character on Lake Michigan during the early 1900s, was a favorite topic when fishermen yarned about bygone days. In 1939, Barkhausen learned that Seavey was still alive and living near Peshtigo,

Henry Barkhausen (right) with the infamous Captain Dan Seavey and Seavey's daughter, Josephine, circa 1945.
WISCONSIN MARITIME MUSEUM

Wisconsin. So, armed with "a steak and a pint of whisky," he drove to Peshtigo and found him living "in a dilapidated farmhouse on hopelessly rundown acreage." Seavey "was very amiable, but suspicious," says Barkhausen. "He was afraid I was going to make a lot of money with a book, but yet he wanted to talk. He talked like water pouring out of a barrel. It was just impossible because I didn't do shorthand. The notes I took in my first visit with Dan [were lost in a house fire in 1994], but he confirmed pretty much his running a floating bordello. He made an impression . . . he was just so immoral. Anyway, it was interesting, but frustrating. I was glad to have met him. I visited with Dan again in early 1940 and in late 1945, with [my wife] Alice."

A LAST CHANCE

In the summer of 1940, Barkhausen booked passage in the 105' *Goldfield,* the last of the wooden Cayman-built gaff-rigged schooners. This vessel, which sailed from Tampa, Florida, to Grand Cayman Island in the Caribbean, was the only means of traveling from the United States to Grand Cayman in those days. The voyage offered him the last chance to sail aboard a traditional schooner. En route to Grand Cayman, radio transmissions picked up by the *Goldfield* announced that Germany had rolled into France. Once back in America, Barkhausen enlisted in the Naval Reserve. After officer training, he returned to civilian life for six months, but when war with Japan seemed imminent, he was called to active duty in June 1941. He and Alice were married the same month.

On December 7, he was aboard a US Navy tanker steaming toward Pearl Harbor with a load of oil when news of the Japanese attack reached the ship. "We were the first ship into Pearl Harbor on Tuesday after the attack," said Barkhausen. "It was just a scene of desolation." Three months later, he was reassigned to a new ship. A week after he left his former one, it was torpedoed and sunk. Barkhausen spent the next four years off New Guinea aboard a PT boat tender and later took over the brand-new Navy cargo ship USS *Bullock* as commanding officer. Coincidentally, *Bullock* was sent back to New Guinea.

Before World War II, *Butcher Boy* was stored during the offseason at the Palmer Johnson shipyard. During the war, the firm built various vessels for the Army and Navy, leaving no space for yacht storage. So, while Barkhausen was in the Pacific, good friends hauled her onto the beach in Oconto, Wisconsin, where she rested under a cover for the duration.

CRUISING THE GREAT LAKES

Returning home in late 1945, Barkhausen went back to work for Northwest Engineering in Green Bay and "was desperate to get on the lake again" in *Butcher Boy*. So, Henry launched her, and he and Alice cruised in her on the Great Lakes until 1950, sailing twice to Lake Superior's North Shore. Conditions aboard were austere, with only a 9' foredeck for shelter. They cooked on an outdoor galley—a portable chest that Barkhausen designed and built. It contained everything necessary for preparing meals, including a small stove.

By the early 1950s, the Barkhausen family had grown to include five children. After chartering another sailboat for several years, Henry commissioned well-known designer Fenwick Williams to draw up a 42' gaff-rigged centerboard schooner—with topsails. The boat, named *Quickstep*, was

Henry Barkhausen in his boat shop in 2014, working on *Final Effort*, a 14' rowing and sailing boat of his own design.
GEORGE D. JEPSON

built on the Chesapeake, and the family sailed her until 1968 when Barkhausen returned to Williams for what he considered the "ultimate cruising boat." The result was *Champion*, a 38' gaff cutter built by Waldo Howland's Concordia Boat Yard in South Dartmouth, Massachusetts. Captain R. D. "Pete" Culler, among the best old-time boatbuilders, also worked on her. The family sailed her until 2007, when Barkhausen donated her to the Maritime Heritage Alliance in Traverse City, Michigan.

Champion was a legend among the upper lakes cruising fraternity, flying a Great Lakes Cruising Club fifty-year membership pennant. Traditionalists to the core, the Barkhausens often sailed into anchorages without using the engine, sometimes in pretty crowded conditions. They also preferred to raise the sail while still at anchor. "We had good tackle, and I could hoist the main by myself, but Alice often came forward to help," explained Henry. "With the halyard under its belaying pin, she would take a strain and take in the slack as I swayed the sail up the last foot or so."

A gaff-topsail was common to all of Barkhausen's cruising boats, harking back to *Butcher Boy*. "The topsail represents the traditional image of older yachts and commercial sail, whether underway or at anchor, with the spars painted white in the doublings," he said. "On *Champion*, it was a very efficient sail. Ours was rigged with both a clewline and buntline, and it could be clewed very snugly when the wind freshened or when anchoring. Of course, I had to go aloft to bend it when fitting out or laying up and occasionally to redo a lashing to the hoops. I was 92 when I last went aloft to bend the topsail."

BUILDING WOODEN BOATS

After moving into a new house in Lake Forest, Illinois, in 1952, Barkhausen embarked on building wooden boats, a pastime that carried through the rest of his life. His first project was a 15'9" crab skiff, designed initially by Captain Charles Edward Leatherbury on the Chesapeake. Next came a 12' tug designed by Fenwick Williams, followed by two sailing dinghies. Finally, as with *Butcher Boy*, he named his sailboats after a Great Lakes schooner. This concluded his building in Lake Forest.

In late 1963, Barkhausen left Northwest Engineering to start a limestone quarry business, settling on a farm south of Jonesboro, Illinois. Summers were spent in Harbor Springs, day-sailing and cruising. Then, in 1981, he retired at age sixty-seven and built a sixty-foot barn with a boat shop inside. His goal was to create a replica of *Butcher Boy* based on

The Barkhausen fleet under sail off Harbor Point at Harbor Springs, Michigan. From left to right the boats are: an unnamed Fred Goeller–designed dinghy; *Rambler*, a 15'6" skipjack taken from an original Ed Leatherbury–designed crab skiff; the Huron boat *Good News*; a 14' Maine peapod; and the tug *Toiler*. COURTESY OF HENRY N. BARKHAUSEN

the lines he had taken back in the late 1930s when he had owned her. Fenwick Williams refined the lines, and Barkhausen lofted the boat.

Christened *Good News*, the new boat was built of solid American timber, including white cedar planking sourced in North Carolina and southern Illinois white oak for the keel and centerboard. The boat was powered with a single-cylinder, Norwegian-built Sabb engine driving a reversible propeller. The project took nine years, with time out to spend summers on Harbor Point. *Good News* was completed in 1990 and launched at Harbor Springs. After that, Barkhausen built a 13' tug called *Toiler*, a salute to the original tug built by Northwest Engineering Company, and a 15'6" skipjack crab skiff, with lines taken from his earlier Ed Leatherbury–designed skiff.

In the summer of 1994, Barkhausen and his son, Henry W., planned to tour Lake Huron and Georgian Bay in *Good News*, visiting places where Mackinaw boats had initially been used commercially. But east of Mackinac Island in northern Lake Huron, fate intervened. "We were forcing it with the engine under sail, and we took a couple of freak waves over the lee bow and swamped it," said Henry. "So that ended that trip and we had to get her hauled back to Irish Boat Shop in Harbor Springs. I couldn't persuade my wife to let me go cruising again in *Good News*."

Over twenty years later, *Good News* remained an iconic reminder of earlier days on the Great Lakes, gracing Little Traverse Bay, and Barkhausen, ready to cross the century mark, was still building

Henry Barkhausen at the helm of *Good News*. **The boat, launched in 1990, is a replica of** *Butcher Boy*, **the transom-sterned Mackinaw boat Barkhausen owned in the 1930s.**
COURTESY OF HENRY N. BARKHAUSEN

wooden boats. After moving back to Lake Forest in 2001, he built a 12' Goeller-designed sailing dinghy, and a 14' Joel White–designed Maine peapod. A new skiff that Barkhausen called *Final Effort* was under construction in 2014.

In 1983, Barkhausen was a principal founder of the Association for Great Lakes Maritime History, an organization of institutions and individuals from both Canada and the United States. That organization's Henry N. Barkhausen Award for Original Research in Great Lakes Maritime History honors his lifelong contributions to preserving the rich history of the Inland Seas.

After our conversation, we climbed into Barkhausen's SUV and drove down the road to the three-stall garage where he was building *Final Effort*, a 14' sailing and rowing skiff of his own design. The little carvel hull rested on stocks, waiting for interior work. Henry beamed in the bright sunshine filtering through the door, his callused hands caressing the wooden gunwale.

On October 6, 2018, Henry Noyes Barkhausen, businessman, sailor, and conservationist, died peacefully at age 103. Alice died on December 10, 2022, a week after her 101st birthday.

SHIPMASTER AND HISTORIAN EDWARD CARUS

Captain Edward Carus was scarcely fourteen years old in 1874 when he shipped aboard the 197' side-wheel steamer *Alpena* as a porter on the run across Lake Michigan from Milwaukee, Wisconsin, to Ludington, Michigan. This launched his career on the Great Lakes, which spanned fifty-five years and eventually led to the command of passenger steamers of the Goodrich Transportation Company fleet. During this period, Carus witnessed the epic transition from stalwart gaff-rigged schooners to great steam-driven ships.

The son of a German exile, Carus was born on April 15, 1860, at Manitowoc, Wisconsin, on Lake Michigan's western shore. A year before the Civil War, Manitowoc had become a thriving seaport and shipbuilding center. The inner harbor teemed with working schooners and steamers belching black smoke from their stacks. Along the shore, shipyards buzzed with activity.

It was the stuff of dreams for boys like Edward Carus, who haunted the Manitowoc waterfront much as Tom Sawyer and Huckleberry Finn had done during the heyday of steamboats on the mighty Mississippi. Carus achieved his dream when he stepped aboard *Alpena* and left formal schooling in his wake. During the next six years, while learning his trade in this steamer, he held berths as both watchman and wheelsman.

Captain Edward Carus, posed here for a formal portrait in 1930, amassed a great collection of Great Lakes artifacts and photographs. Henry Barkhausen acquired Carus's archives after Carus's death in 1947 and continued to build on them. Barkhausen eventually donated the collection to the Wisconsin Maritime Museum. CARUS COLLECTION, WISCONSIN MARITIME MUSEUM

In 1880, Carus shipped before the mast in a pair of 172' three-masted schooners, the *C. C. Barnes* and the *Samuel J. Tilden.* The following year, now with a master's license, he returned to steamers, serving as the second mate and then mate in a succession of vessels, including the 172' propeller-driven *Corona* and the 171' propeller-driven *Joseph L. Hurd.* His first command was the small packet steamer, *Nellie,* in 1887, which carried the US mail between Harbor

Springs, Michigan, and the offshore Beaver Islands in Lake Michigan. Carus later captained several Goodrich Steamship Line vessels, including the 208' side-wheeler *Sheboygan* and the 180' propeller-driven *City of Ludington,* renamed *Georgia* in 1898. During his career, Carus collected over three thousand rare photographs of Great Lakes ships and gathered their written histories, models, and records depicting their accomplishments and tragedies. He preserved the collection in the "Pilot House," a room in his modest cottage near the Manitowoc shipyards.

After retiring in 1929, Carus wrote and illustrated a series of articles for the Manitowoc *Herald-Times* about Great Lakes ships, which were based on material in his collection. Henry Barkhausen acquired the archives from Carus (who died in 1947), continued to build upon them, and donated the collection to the Wisconsin Maritime Museum in 1981. In the years after, Barkhausen presented the institution with more original builders' models, rare paintings, lithographs, and books.

Many rare photographs from the Carus Collection were included in the book *Great Lakes Sailing Ships,* written by Henry Barkhausen in 1947. It was the second volume in the *Ships and Sailing Albums* series published by Kalmbach Publishing. The Manitowoc *Herald-Times* articles are available at www.Newspapers.com. The Carus Collection of photographs has been digitized through a gift from Barkhausen and may be accessed online at www.wisconsinmaritime.org.

The *Lady Isabel* (42' LOA, 10' beam, and 43" draft) was launched in 1907 at the H. B. Burger shipyard in Manitowoc, Wisconsin. She was designed by Edson B. Schock with a round bottom and canoe stern to better handle the choppy waters of the Great Lakes. My grandfather purchased her in 1946 in Green Bay, Wisconsin, and sailed her across Lake Michigan into Lake Huron, up the St. Mary's River, through the Soo Locks, and to Marquette on Lake Superior. AUTHOR'S COLLECTION

Afterword

The years spent researching and writing the original *WoodenBoat* articles and, more recently, adding to them for *Sailing the Sweetwater Seas,* rekindled treasured memories dating back to my formative years on Lake Superior enthralled with the long-ships, or "ore boats," passing through Marquette. The Big Lake—Gitche Gumee—immortalized by Henry Wadsworth Longfellow in "The Song of Hiawatha" and, later, by Gordon Lightfoot with his ballad, "Wreck of the Edmund Fitzgerald," seduced me long ago.

As a young boy in Marquette, I often sat in McCarty's Cove on summer days, spellbound by Superior's many moods. It was a stone's throw from my grandparents' home. The waves were sometimes angry and stormy, other times gently breaking on the sugar-sand beach beside the iconic light-house, which dates back to 1866, replacing the first light that became operational in 1853 but quickly deteriorated.

These were the years immediately after World War II. There was no television yet in Michigan's Upper Peninsula due, we were told, to the iron ore ranges affecting signals. So, to entertain myself, I read comic books, listened to adventure programs on the radio, and spent as much time as possible at Marquette's Lower Harbor. My grandfather, George Henderson Jepson, moored his 42' vintage wooden motor yacht, *Lady Isabel*—built in 1907 in Manitowoc, Wisconsin—at Max Reynolds's Lake Superior Yacht Yard. Reynolds, a retired million-aire who had made his fortune in the powder industry during World War I, built his private yard with a boathouse, carpenter shop, and marine railway to service his sleek, black 52', two-masted schooner *Yankee Girl.*

I often tagged along with Gramp to the boat-yard. Each spring, he worked on the *Lady Isabel,* warmed by a charcoal stove in the Upper Penin-sula's typically cold climate. His cheek frequently bulged with a chaw of tobacco, or he had an unlit cigar stub clamped between his teeth. In summers, the boat was moored in the harbor just off the yard. Cruising or fishing for lake trout with our family on Lake Superior, with its deep blue hues on sunny days, was a delight.

After we moved to Lower Michigan in 1951, I spent summer vacations with my grandparents in Marquette. I learned to row in the harbor. And after he built a cabin cruiser called *Idleour*, replacing *Lady Isabel*, I had stints at the helm. Boats were my passion. The first fall away from Marquette, my second-grade teacher caught me staring out the window and asked what was on my mind. "My grandfather's boat," I sheepishly replied. She smiled and suggested I pay attention to our penmanship lesson as we worked with lined paper that had wooden slivers embedded in it and wrote with chunky wooden pencils.

Decades later, the scent of fresh wood shavings and a crackling fire in Reynolds's carpenter shop, where the "old-timers" chewed, smoked, and swapped stories, conjure up vivid memories. *Lady Isabel* and *Yankee Girl* were my first crushes.

This photo shows my grandfather, George Henderson Jepson (left), and my father, George Lewis Jepson, aboard the *Lady Isabel* in 1946. Father and son chartered the boat for deep-sea fishing parties on Lake Superior after Dad returned from the South Pacific and duty aboard US Army Air Force crash boats during World War II. AUTHOR'S COLLECTION

Happily, the *Lady Isabel*, fully restored to its 1940s appearance, is permanently on display at the Wisconsin Maritime Museum near her birthplace in Manitowoc over a century ago. She is the oldest known boat built by H. B. Burger.

Across Marquette's Lower Harbor, a massive ore dock rose beside a wharf where commercial fish tugs moored when they weren't out on the lake. Ore boats loaded taconite pellets on both sides of the dock. And periodically, the luxury passenger

David G. Syren, my maternal grandfather, was the senior engineer on the LS&I railroad. As a lad, I was thrilled to watch him moving railroad cars filled with taconite to load ore boats on the Presque Isle Dock in Marquette, carrying on a process that had begun a century earlier in the first iron ore port on the Great Lakes. AUTHOR'S COLLECTION

steamship *South American*—314' in length, with a 47' beam and drawing 18'—stopped at Marquette during cruises on Lake Superior. As a result, the harbor was generally abuzz with activity.

The ore dock on the Upper Harbor—also known as the Presque Isle Dock—was one of my favorite places because my maternal grandfather, David Syren, was the senior engineer for the LS&I Railroad. He had immigrated to America from Sweden in 1914, arriving in New York aboard the liner *Lusitania* a year before a German U-boat torpedoed and sunk her in the Irish Sea. So watching him, with his traditional pin-striped engineer's cap, at the controls of a steam locomotive, pushing cars carrying taconite out onto the ore dock to load ships, was always a thrill.

At the time, I was oblivious to our family's deeper Great Lakes maritime history, which dates back to the previous century. And then, on a late summer morning in 1953, with warm showers drifting in off Lake Michigan, our family, including my dad's parents, were in Charlevoix on Michigan's northwest coast. As we slowly wandered down Michigan Avenue, fronting the harbor, Gramps glanced in an antiques shop window and saw a large, framed photograph of the steamer *Hum*. Minutes later, he emerged from the shop with the picture under his arm. Listening to the adults discuss the photo, I

This photo of the Jepson steamer *Hum*, with him barely visible in the pilothouse, was discovered by George Henderson Jepson, in a Charlevoix, Michigan, shop in the early 1950s. **AUTHOR'S COLLECTION**

yearned to learn more about the steamer and, more specifically, about Gramp's life. But sadly, he died unexpectedly soon after, and our lives changed. By then, living in Lower Michigan, where Dad had a new position as a chemical engineer, other interests intervened. So, as the years passed, those joyous days in Marquette and thoughts of the *Hum* were pleasant but distant memories—until I queried Matt Murphy about the schooner article.

At about the same time, I was researching our family genealogy and discovered that the Jepsons had immigrated from England, but not in a conventional way. It turned out that my great-great-grandfather, Joseph Jepson, had arrived in Upper Canada (part of modern-day Ontario) in 1843 with Queen Victoria's 82nd Regiment of Foot (Prince of Wales's Volunteers) after serving at Gibraltar and the West Indies. While stationed at Penetanguishene, a small community on Lake Huron's Georgian Bay, he married Eliza Henderson and started a family. In the early 1850s, separated from the British army, the Jepsons, likely traveling by steamer, immigrated to Green Bay, Wisconsin. By 1860, the family had grown to five children, including my great-grandfather, George, who had been born in 1851. In October 1861, Joseph marched off with the Wisconsin 12th Infantry during the Civil War, never to return. Sadly, he died from illness in July 1863 and was buried at Benton Barracks in St. Louis, Missouri. A decade later, George, in his early twenties, had moved to Chicago and sailed in the schooner trade on Lake Michigan like many immigrants from his generation. At the same time, his brother, Joseph, served as a porter aboard passenger steamers.

By the early 1880s, George—after that known as Captain Jepson—skippered his own schooner, the 67', two-masted *Mamie Jepson*, sailing from Manistee on Michigan's northwest shore. Later in the decade, Captain Jepson had transitioned from schooners to steamers, founding the East Jordan and Charlevoix Line. It was late in my grandfather's life when I learned that he—known then as young George—had captained the *Hum* until 1917, after his father's untimely death in 1905. And during the 1940s, my father, George Lewis Jepson, was licensed to "operate and navigate motorboats carrying passengers for hire" on the Great Lakes.

So, the sweetwater seas run through our family. In the beginning, as I researched and wrote the original articles for *WoodenBoat*, I relied on my years around the Great Lakes for starting points. And as *Sailing the Sweetwater Seas* came together, I mined newly available digitized newspaper articles about contemporary events, bringing them alive as they happened. In those days, telegrams from various points around the Lakes sent to publications like *The Inter Ocean* in Chicago and local newspapers kept readers informed of the whereabouts of various vessels and, sadly, disasters.

The Chicago Daily Tribune report on October 8, 1884, about *Mamie Jepson,* caught in a storm on Lake Michigan, rekindled a personal memory of a similar experience nearly a century later. In the summer of 1975, with three others, I crewed aboard a 30' sloop sailing south on Lake Michigan from Charlevoix to Holland on Michigan's western shore. It was a voyage I would never forget. The lake is particularly dangerous when storms strike from northerly directions, allowing them to sweep the open body of water.

Clearing the Charlevoix South Pier Lighthouse in the early evening, we skirted Grand Traverse Bay and rounded Cat Head Point as the sun set across the lake in Wisconsin. Down the coast, we overnighted in Leland and sailed farther south to Pentwater the following day. At Pentwater, a front moved into the region, weathering us in for two days. Clay Sherman, a fellow crewman, and I spent several hours in a cafe near the harbor, shooting pool to the strains of America's "Sister Golden Hair" repeatedly playing on the jukebox.

Believing the latest forecast that the worst was over, we sailed again two mornings later, hoping to make Holland in one run. But, as we tacked south out of Pentwater, the sloop beat into a southerly, kicking up the waters in the dangerous, shoaled Manitou Passage, making life aboard uncomfortable. By mid-afternoon, the sky turned a dirty, yellowish pea green after tacking farther into the lake, and the winds steadily increased to 30 miles per hour. Then, suddenly, we heard a loud cracking sound, and the boom swung wildly, breaking loose from the mast. The gooseneck fitting had failed.

So we dropped the mainsail. Motoring was an option, but we made minimal headway in the seas, building to twenty feet. The jib (or foresail) was left flying to help stabilize the boat's motion. As darkness approached, the seas towered over us. The boat crested one wave after another and rapidly slid down into the trough. Our greatest fear was broaching or turning sideways, which would have been disastrous. Gratefully, the wind began to moderate by midnight, and we were sledding southward with a somewhat easier motion. Finally, at about 4:00 a.m., the South Pierhead Lighthouse at Muskegon appeared off our port bow. In short order, we dropped the jib and motored past the light between the piers into Muskegon Lake's calm waters and anchored. We were all exhausted and relieved that our twenty-hour ordeal was over. Although that fateful day occurred over forty years ago, I can still feel the boat's movement and Lake Michigan's immense power.

So, as I approached the articles for *WoodenBoat*, these memories all played a part as I learned about the mariners who braved the sweetwater seas aboard wooden boats and ships designed and built by local shipwrights on their shores. Along the way, discovering more of our family's history on the Great Lakes was an unexpected gift.

Selected Bibliography

Bamford, Don. *Freshwater Heritage: A History of Sail on the Great Lakes, 1670–1918.* Toronto: Natural Heritage Books, 2007.

Barkhausen, Henry N. *Focusing on the Centerboard.* Manitowoc: Wisconsin Maritime Museum, 1990.

Barkhausen, Henry N. *Great Lakes Sailing Ships.* Milwaukee: Kalmbach Publishing Company, 1947.

Barkhausen, Henry N. *How a Great Lakes Schooner Was Built in the 1850s.* Manitowoc: Anchor News (Wisconsin Maritime Museum), Fall 2011.

Barkhausen, Henry N. *The Riddle of the Naubinway Sands.* Association for Great Lakes Maritime History, 1947, 1991.

Barkhausen, Henry N. *The Voyage of the Schooner Dean Richmond from Chicago to Liverpool in 1856.* Manitowoc: Anchor News (Wisconsin Maritime Museum), Spring 2011.

Barry, James P. *Ships of the Great Lakes.* Holt, MI: Thunder Bay Press, 1996.

Bazzill, Dina M. *The Missing Link Between Sail and Steam: Steam Barges and the Joys of Door County, Wisconsin.* East Carolina University Research Report No. 19, 2007.

Cameron, Scott L. *The Francis Smith—Palace Steamer of the Upper Great Lakes 1867–1896.* Toronto: Natural Heritage Books, 2005.

Chapelle, Howard I. *The History of American Sailing Ships.* New York: W.W. Norton & Company, Inc., 1935.

Dennis, Jerry. *The Living Great Lakes.* New York: Thomas Dunne Books, 2003.

Devendorf, John F. *Great Lakes Bulk Carriers 1869–1985.* South Bend, IN: Apollo Print & Graphics Center, 1996.

Dickens, Charles. *American Notes for General Circulation.* New York: Penguin Classics, 2001.

Forster, John. *The Life of Charles Dickens.* Google Books, 2010.

Gjerset, Knut. *Norwegian Sailors on the Great Lakes.* New York: Arno Press, 1970.

Hannay, David. *The Life of Frederick Marryat.* Tucson: Fireship Press, 2009.

Havighurst, Walter. *The Long Ships Passing.* Minneapolis: University of Minnesota Press, 1975.

Hilton, George W. *Lake Michigan Passenger Steamers.* Redwood City, CA: Stanford University Press, 2002.

Inches, H. C. *The Great Lakes Wooden Shipbuilding Era.* Privately published, 1962.

Karamanski, Theodore J. *Mastering the Inland Seas.* Madison: University of Wisconsin Press, 2020.

Karamanski, Theodore J. *Schooner Passage: Sailing Ships and the Lake Michigan Frontier.* Detroit: Wayne State University Press, 2001.

Lafferty, William, and Valerie van Heest. *Buckets and Belts—Evolution of the Great Lakes Self-Unloader.* Holland, MI: In-Depth Editions, 2009.

Marryat, Frederick. *Diary in America.* Create Space Independent, 2015.

McGreevy, Robert. *Lost Legends of the Lakes*. Holt, MI: Thunder Bay Press Michigan, 2011.

Neuschel, Fred. *Lives and Legends of the Christmas Tree Ships*. Ann Arbor: University of Michigan Press, 2007.

Nute, Grace Lee. *Lake Superior*. Minneapolis: University of Minnesota Press, 2000.

Richardson, Ross. *The Search for the* Westmoreland: *Lake Michigan's Treasure Shipwreck*. Traverse City, MI: Arbutus Press, 2012.

St. Mane, Ted. *Lost Passenger Steamers of Lake Michigan*. Charleston, SC: History Press, 2010.

Sherman, Elizabeth. *Beyond the Windswept Dunes: The Story of Maritime Muskegon*. Detroit: Wayne State University Press, 2003.

Van Heest, Valerie. *Lost on the Lady Elgin*. Holland, MI: In-Depth Editions, 2010.